It's Just a Matter of Balance

Kevin S. Garrison

Quality Printing Services

2005

ISBN 0-9773261-0-1

51995

9 780977 326105

$19.95

Cover Photography
SIGNATURE Photography By ARNIE
Davie, Florida
axelfl@aol.com

Cover Design
Marvin Kravitz

Please send all inquiries and book orders to:

Garrison's Prosthetic Services, Inc.
17184 N.E. 19th Avenue
North Miami Beach, Florida 33162 USA

www.oandp.com/garrison's

Published for the author by:

Print Vantage
2111 South Green Road
South Euclid, OH 44121

www.printvantage.com

Dedication

I am dedicating this book to all those brave souls who have endured so much and yet refuse to give up on the pursuit of their dreams - the happy survivors!

A portion of the proceeds from the sale of this book will be donated to **The Barr Foundation**. This foundation assists amputees who have no funding, making the realization of a prosthetic device possible for those so in need.

* The names have been changed to protect the privacy of the individuals.

Acknowledgements

The greatest of thanks to my wife, Catheline, for all her most loving and encouraging help. I want to thank my mother and father, also Marsha and Judy for all of their helpful guidance.

Contents

Introduction

"It's in us all"

I feel that the human being is a remarkable biological combination of cells, resulting in a masterpiece of development, you and me! I am sure the greatest thinkers of our rich past contemplated, on a regular basis, the remarkable abilities they found in themselves as well as those around them. The things we take for granted each day which come to us so easily, just cannot be accomplished by all the inhabitants of our beautiful planet individually.

We have in us the ability to adapt to any situation or specific goal when given the time and opportunity to study our new circumstances of life, should they suddenly change. We then can slowly adjust *if we choose to*.

All of us can adapt to climate change relating to intense physical exertion to our bodies. Artistic control of our wrists, hands and fingers for musical instruments and paintbrushes can also be accomplished over time. Coordination of all our limbs for managing machinery of all types and even great sporting activities can also be accomplished with repetitive effort and determination.

Achieving the goal can be done if we choose to adapt and then follow through by maintaining this determination which is so necessary for success, and in some cases downright survival. It can be done!

I felt compelled to share my story because I firmly believe in the human race as a race of very strong beings, both physically as well as mentally. The fact that we still exist is to me alone a testament to that belief! As humans we are unfortunately subjected to all forms of potential damage to our health during our lives. Physical and mental problems can occur through disease or traumatic accidents as well as social events and aging. It's just our basic human frailties and imperfections reacting to the challenges of life, and the risks we all take every day, that allow us to get hurt or to possibly become permanently disabled.

If we become disabled, we must embrace our disability with this fantastic unique inner strength that we all possess within us. Using the genuine acceptance of our fate, we can then begin to truly live out our days to the fullest, as we all deserve.

Enjoy your gift of life to the fullest!

Prologue

"The Celebration"

"Where is the guest list?" asked Sophia, the young, talented woman we had hired to help us plan a joyous celebration. The party was to be in honor of Kevin's 30th anniversary of his prosthetic career. As we sat around the coffee table, Sophia continued to ask questions about the menu, guest attire, flower arrangements and Flamenco music, Kevin's favorite. I couldn't help glancing across the family room and catching Kevin's deep and profound look as he stared at the simple, yet elegant party invitation Sophia and I had created.

Sophia and I had been working on this event for many weeks. I absolutely wanted to make sure the theme of the party would reflect the joyous nature of this splendid occasion for Kevin as well as our family and friends. We carefully reviewed the verbiage on the invitation ensuring it fully expressed the details of the celebration. We also made sure there were no errors in the printing. We carefully checked and re-checked every detail. Oh the details! The evening was going to be perfect, I kept saying to myself.

When we first met, I had told Sophia that this party we were planning is about a very special accomplishment in our lives as a family. We wanted to celebrate and to give thanks and honor so many of our patients, friends, and family who had trusted and embraced Kevin and me in our quest to assist amputees. I especially wanted Kevin to know how proud I am of him. I am proud of his perseverance and determination to follow his dreams no matter what.

As I fidgeted with the papers she had just handed me, Sophia kept reminding me that the celebration was less than three weeks away. So many details, so little time, Sophia kept saying as she looked over the music contract and repertoire of Kevin's most favorite Flamenco music. I couldn't help notice from a distance, his distinctive and very familiar change in posture.

As I speculated as to why his demeanor seemed to gradually change, Kevin continued to sip on his first cup of freshly brewed ground Jamaican Blue Mountain coffee. He loved his coffee; two cups in the early morning savored slowly. I watched him as he contemplated Mother Nature at her best; he gazed at the combinations of colorful saltwater fish in our aquarium. Watching him enjoy the playful nature of our four Maine Coon cats as they came to sit with him while he continues to take pleasure in his coffee, is my special delight to study.

The cooing of Rosie and Poncho, our colorful Macaw parrots, is the background music of the early morning in our home. Mother Nature really speaks to you in Florida, especially in our backyard as the sun comes up. We enjoy the peaceful view out our windows, gazing at all the lush variations of green, from the darkest shades of the palm fronds, to the lightest tropical feathery plant leaves. During most of the year we enjoy all the vibrant flowering hibiscus and bougainvillea plants of yellow, pink and deep purple.

This morning was different. I couldn't help but notice the subtle tilting of Kevin's head and the nervous movements of his foot as he crossed it over his leg. He held the ivory-colored party invitation with beautiful flowing gold script lettering very carefully with his right hand, as if to seriously review it. Yet, I felt his thoughts were elsewhere.

I put the papers that were in my hand down on the table, leaving Ms. Sophia as she mumbled some indistinguishable words under her breath. I walked over to my beloved husband. I moved slowly past the cozy chenille sectional sofa in the family room and then toward the warm and inviting breakfast nook where he was sitting quietly. The morning sunlight washed the walls with hues of amber; the expansive lake view was serine and spectacular this early morning. The fresh ground coffee aroma continued to fill the air. Our four dogs, which completed our children, ran playfully in our backyard chasing each other as I viewed them.

"Kevin," I said. "Do you like it?" I didn't let him answer before I nervously asked him again, this time with greater excitement. "Isn't it perfect?" There was a quiet moment. As he turned to look at me, I noticed his normally stoic face had changed to a definite expression of what I would call the look of gentle contentment. His brown, somewhat tired watery eyes had a kind of sparkle to them as he began to smile modestly. I saw a tear falling from his cheek. He sat saying no words, yet I knew what his silent words were as if he was speaking them out loud to me softly. The words describing his story flashed in front of me; his life, our life, and our destiny together. In that moment I thought of this bright, strong, athletic teenaged boy who lost his most precious possessions; his right foot, his body image, his balance. Yet I know for a fact he had never lost his dreams. I was startled, yet I did feel at peace when I heard my husband say, "Perfect, Catheline, it is perfect."

Catheline L. Garrison JD, OTR/L

Chapter 1

In the Beginning

"We feel you have a ninety-five percent chance of having your right foot amputated due to the reoccurrence of the tumor," he said. I was quiet for some very long seconds. Tears welled in the corners of my eyes. The pit of my stomach tightened, and I almost shook with emotion. I just wanted to leave that exam room. Surely if I just left, everything would go back to normal. Those horrible words with their gruesome image would go away, if only I could get out of the hospital. I just wanted to leave, I thought, as the panicked feeling grew worse. I'm not dealing with this. I'm not going to come back to this hospital, I thought, as I started feeling more in control.

The summer heat baked the streets of El Paso, Texas, cooking the tar in the road until it began to bubble. The brown grass yearned for the cooling rains. When the rains finally came, the grass grew lush and green, creating summer fun for my friends and me. The summer of 1969 was especially hot, so we treasured the rain and the simple pleasures it brought.

When the rains came, we would run to the park and watch as the water came slithering down from the top of the majestic, light brown, rain-soaked mountain, forming a pool on the playing fields. My friends and I would take our shoes off and run as fast as we possibly could, jump and slide, hydroplaning over the thick dark green grass, falling, rolling and getting soaking wet. I will never forget the sweet smell of the wet grass in the park, inhaling it with my nose so close to the ground and the air with the heavy scent from the wet desert sand surrounding us, saturated like musk everywhere. It was wonderful. I ran and jumped and slid that day until I was exhausted, stopping only after smacking my right foot into a small flat rock just under the water's surface. I sat down and saw that the toe next to my big toe was swollen. I'll tell you it hurt like hell, but of course I had to hide that from my friends. After all, we were only sixteen years old and we were very tough kids. After the initial pain subsided, I pretended that I had to get home. I walked the one block home looking forward to resting in my bedroom. I studied my toe for the next few days and learned to walk in such a way that it didn't hurt too much. However, whenever I would forget, my toe would eagerly remind me with a shooting pain. I came to the conclusion that I had broken the bone that attaches the toe to the foot, as it just stayed swollen. The swelling remained even after it finally stopped hurting.

However, being sixteen, I ignored my swollen toe. There were so many things that were more interesting. The desert for one. It was so intriguing, so much nature just down at the end of our street. My friends and I often went on all day hiking trips. We would look for fossils of ancient ocean animals that had died millions of years ago. Most often we only stumbled upon faded, colored pieces of broken Indian pottery hundreds of years old. Holding those bits of history in my hand was just a wild experience for me. I felt a physical connection to life in the near and far past. All around us were wild animals; lizards with ringed tails in all different sizes and colors; lonely coyotes trotted along in the distant horizon. Doves, quail, jackrabbits and roadrunners were as common as the cool breezes. Scorpions, rattlesnakes, and other strange poisonous creatures crept along the brown desert ground. While contact with those organisms was always a possibility, we tried to avoid them. We loved to go out deep into the ever-expanding desert wilderness and forget all our problems. When the winter days grew short and the weather was cold, we would cook out in the desert. Yes, we would bring water, a cooking pot, salt, pepper, matches and enough eggs so we could each have two. Boiling up those eggs over a Mesquite wood fire, arguing over who was going to get the cracked ones, feeling hungry and anticipating our most exceptional meal, was wonderful. Eventually, we actually ate the eggs while we sat in the brown desert sand. We enjoyed them so, as they were always so excellent. There is nothing like eating desert-cooked boiled eggs in the winter desert of El Paso.

Winter turned to spring, and months later I was watching T.V. one morning with no shoes on and my mom saw my right foot and noticed that swollen toe. By now there was a bump at the base of the toe that extended to my foot. My mother took one look at it and declared that something was wrong and it needed to be checked by the doctor. I think she was upset that she hadn't noticed it earlier. I told her that it was nothing; I was fine. I had rationalized that the bump must have been caused at the same time as the toe break, back when I kicked the rock playing in that outrageous field with my friends. The swollen toe and bump were simply some type of a delayed reaction. My mom wasn't accepting any of my explanations. "We're going to the doctor and that foot is getting checked," she said and to the doctor we went.

After the exam, Dr. Goldner, whom I had known since I was ten, agreed with Mom that it looked like something was going on in there. The x-ray revealed a cavity or hole in the bone of the toe. Dr. Goldner wanted me to see a specialist, an orthopedic doctor, to find out what had happened to the toe. We then saw Dr. Bassett, whose office was in the same building. After one look at the toe and the x-rays, Dr. Bassett wanted to perform surgery in order to go into the toe bone and scrape off samples of the bone tissue to test.

Surgery was set up immediately. I remember getting wheeled into the operating room area while lying on my

3

back. I saw my name on a board up high on the wall with an "L" with a circle around it next to my name. I called a nurse over and asked her if that "L" meant my left foot and proceeded to explain that the problem was in my right foot. She then seemed to ignore me as they had already given me a shot of something to relax me and I probably didn't know what I was talking about. I apparently kept going on about it because the doctor came into the room and looked at both my feet under the bright white sheet and corrected the notation. I think someone must have gotten in trouble for that little oversight. The doctor told my parents that he didn't like the look of what they found, although there was no cancer present in what they tested. He wanted us to go see some experts on this type of phenomena to make sure that everything was okay and my strange looking toe wasn't hiding anything sinister. We were then sent to the city of Houston, Texas, to see the specialists in a hospital called "M.D. Anderson Tumor and Research Center." I was sure that these experts would figure it out and tell my parents that what had happened to my foot was really nothing serious. I knew all along that it was nothing!

Chapter 2

Houston, my First Medical Visit

The doctors immediately wanted to test the tissue on the top of the bone in my foot where the bump was so they could determine what exactly it was. There were several doctors involved. One doctor even asked permission to take pictures of my foot, as this was something they had never seen before. I thought this was cool; I was going to be in a medical book; well my foot anyway! Dr. Bengerman did say that the biopsy wouldn't hurt because I would get an injection of Novocain in the skin before they cut through it. I couldn't believe that a simple injection of Novocain would prevent the pain that a sharp knife cutting through my skin to the bone was bound to inflict and I became very tense. However, I went into the room like the brave soul that I was and proceeded to lie on my back as directed on this weird looking flat table like a bed in the room's center. This was definitely some type of operating room because it looked so different. They should call this room the Antarctica chrome room I thought, because everything except the ceiling and floor was coated with chrome. Just entering the room gave me a cold feeling. Lying on my back with my right leg all exposed, I felt as if I was in a refrigerator. I actually started to shiver slightly and my teeth began to vibrate and chatter uncontrollably.

Dr. Bengerman came into the room. From my perspective on the table he seemed very tall and a little scary, masked and garbed for the procedure. He reassured me again that it wouldn't hurt. I still didn't believe him. He was an intern or student doctor who was instructed by the main surgeon assigned to me, Dr. Green, to perform this procedure. I focused on the chrome light fixture attached to the ceiling directly in my view, trying to blot out what was

5

happening to me. The pinch of the Novocain-filled needle hurt as it penetrated the skin. It hurt a lot. It hurt every time he pulled it out and pushed it in again and again.

However, Dr. Bengerman was right and I didn't feel much of the actual cutting. In fact, everything was fine until he started pressing down firmly with some type of scissors, snipping at an edge of the bump in an effort to remove a piece for testing. I cringed when I heard a piece of the hard material ting against the metal light fixture that hung directly over the work area. That clink made everything too real. I couldn't wait for the procedure to end. I began fidgeting as electrical shock waves shot up my leg every time he firmly pressed down. After what seemed to be an eternity, he finally sensed that what he was doing was killing me and he abruptly stopped what he was doing. I was so thankful that he stopped. He finished by putting in seven stitches, pulling the cut skin together in a crescent moon-shaped line. Dr. Bengerman told me I had done a great job and thanked me as he then left the room. It was over. I was exhausted. The nurse brought me back to my mom. Mom took one look at my face and knew I had just gone through hell. She looked sad and very concerned about me as she spoke to the doctor for a few minutes. We left the hospital and went to my cousins' house where we were staying while we were in Houston. Mom told me that we would be coming back the next day to discuss the test results and the plans that would follow.

My foot hurt all night and most of the next day, much to my naïve surprise. However, I didn't want my mother to worry too much, so I acted as if the foot didn't hurt as much as it did. You see my mother is a professional worrier and I have always felt uncomfortable seeing her distressed, angry or sad.

The next day Dr. Bengerman told Mom and me that he believed that the bump was a small growth. He went on to say that it should be removed along with the toe and connecting bone that it surrounded in my foot. He told us that even though the growth was not cancerous, it should still be removed. Arrangements for surgery were quickly made. I slowly began to realize that I was to lose a toe.

Once more I was being wheeled to surgery, only this time I was going down a long narrow hallway with big bright rectangular white lights pasted on the ceiling; one on the right and one on the left caddy corner to each other, one after the other after the other all the way to the stopping point that apparently was at the end of this super-stretched, never-ending hallway. As I took that unbelievable, long, surrealistic ride to the place where toes were removed, (the "surgery suite") I was feeling the weird sensation of the injection they had just given me. The last thing I remember was the doors slamming behind me as I drifted into unconsciousness.

When I awoke, I saw my mom at my side. I began to smile, but pain exploded in my foot and the smile turned to a grimace. I felt as if I was being chased and the pain was catching up with me with a final boom. I knew then that Dr. Green must have definitely done what he said he was going to do! My foot was buried under inches of gauze wrappings so I wasn't able to see exactly what he had done. But I could feel it. It was a rough couple of days!

My hospital room could accommodate four patients, although there were only two guys already in there. The cramped room had tan colored metal bed frames and headboards, tan colored walls, chairs and cabinets. A thin dark tan curtain was draped halfway around my space, giving a slight sense of privacy. I was happy to be next to the window even though I could not see anything out there. The natural beauty of the outside light and sky showering over me as I lay helplessly in my bed made me feel a little better. The natural light gave me a warm feeling of health and well-being or maybe it was just the pain medication doing that.

I think my roommates were worse to deal with than the actual pain of the surgery. One late night this old guy in the bed next to me who was always unconscious must have been given the wrong brownish milkshake type stuff in his feeding tube. He started passing gas late that night. The noise and stench from the tremendous gas attack that he was having was so disgusting that it jarred me awake, despite all the medication that I had received. The room smelled so bad that I could not breathe. I didn't care how sick he was. I just wanted him to stop emitting that suffocating odor. I was desperate to make him stop and began thinking menacing thoughts, like moving his bed out in the hallway or out of the hospital altogether! Well since I couldn't physically do that I wondered what I could do? Finally I decided to buzz the nurse. Choking, I tried to explain to the nurse over the intercom, that I was suffocating from the exhaust fumes produced by my roommate who had been given some type of spoiled liquid nourishment for his last meal. She didn't understand me and I was too nice of a kid or maybe just too shy, to try and explain in more detail, so I just breathed through my pillow for a while. After all, I figured he had to stop some time, you know, eventually run out of gas.

Then there was a kid my age in the bed directly across from mine who had lost his leg above the knee from cancer. He wore a knitted dark blue hat all the time because he had no hair. I never really spoke to him but I had to know why he didn't have any hair on his head. Mom was my private investigator and she found out everything, actually more than we wanted to know. He was dying. His chemotherapy was not working. It had no effect on the aggressive cancer, but it made him lose all his hair.

He made me feel very uneasy. He was bald. He was dying. He was just a few feet away from me. Looking at him made me wonder if I would lose my hair. It's funny; I was never worried about or even thought about dying.

My mom had the doctor talk to me. Dr. Bengerman told me that my hair wasn't going anywhere and not to worry about it. I felt very embarrassed as he talked to me about it. But my mom was there to alleviate any of my fears and take care of me the best that she could; you see that's my mom, always taking care of her sons.

I spent three very long weeks in the hospital. The doctors had pulled tendons over the void that they had made in my foot during the surgery. They stretched my skin over the area, but the skin was not taking the abuse very well. It literally looked black. Later I found out that the doctors were considering doing a skin graft if the skin didn't heal quickly enough. The skin had to heal before I could be sent back home. It seemed as if I had to wait forever.

I remember one nice nurse named Emily who had a truly angelic, peaceful smile. She liked my artwork and encouraged me to draw to pass the time. She was very beautiful. I gave her some of my best handiwork. I had a new set of grease pencils that had every color of the rainbow in it. I used every color at my disposal and my artistic ability to create scenes of the city and the countryside. I drew animals and people in an effort to pass the time and keep busy. I had taken art classes in my freshman, sophomore, and junior years and was planning to take one again my senior year. My art teacher considered me one of her advanced students and gave me more challenging art projects than the other students each year. I found my talent and her instruction very helpful as I struggled to keep my mind off my problems.

Nurse Emily encouraged me to leave my room and explore the hospital grounds. Early one evening she told me to travel around the hospital in my wheelchair to get some exercise and change my view. I told her I was embarrassed to have strangers see me. I was sure that they would stare at my strange, ugly-looking foot, with its blackened top, sutures, and missing toe, as it stuck out in front of me like some strange battering ram. Emily quickly discouraged this notion. "You're in a hospital and that's the kind of thing people see in a hospital. Don't be silly, just go," she said.

Hesitantly I rolled myself out of my room. No one stopped and stared. They were all too busy with their own issues. The hallways seemed huge to me, with shiny polished green floors, and bright lights reflecting off the yellow walls. The constant smell of antiseptics and alcohol permeated the air like a thick, floating, invisible mass. If people wanted to look at my foot they did; if they didn't want to look, they didn't. I started feeling a little more confident.

Traveling down an adjacent hallway after making two right turns, I discovered the room of the pro football player who had just lost his leg high above the knee due to cancer. He was the hospital's local celebrity. His room was filled with many different colored flowers. Flowers were on the floor and stacked on all the furniture in his private room. Even though the lights in his room were dimmed, I noticed that he saw me out in the brightly lit hallway. I was too shy to talk or to dare interrupt his privacy, so I just wheeled myself away slowly.

I adjusted out of necessity or to just survive. Three weeks in the hospital was a claustrophobic experience on many levels. I was very happy to have Emily with me during the night shift and, of course, my mom was always with me during the day.

One night Emily, my favorite nurse, told me that she used to be a nun. Her angelic aura, her powdery white, pretty, soft, smiling face, short jet-black hair and light blue eyes made her seem like a gift from God. I don't know why she wasn't a nun any more, but I was glad she was *my* nurse.

I appreciated her gentle kindness and genuine concern for my feelings during this confusing and angry time in my life.

Sometimes during the afternoons I would sit with my mom in a small wooded area on the edge of the hospital's parking lot. I ate Cheetos® and fed them to the squirrels while we would enjoy the crisp breeze of the late afternoon. Mom and I talked about different things, but mostly I drove her crazy complaining about my confinement in this prison hospital for what felt like an eternity. She would do her best to console me and give me advice on how to best cope with my predicament in a healthy way. I had no patience to listen to helpful advice from my mother. I wanted to go home! I was miserable. I was being very selfish though because I was the one preventing her from being with my dad and brothers for such a long time! Like a typical teenager, I dismissed her feelings because this was all happening to me. Finally the day came. I was free to return home to my dad, brothers and friends who, much to my surprise, I had missed very much.

Chapter 3

Going Back to School

I wasn't sure how the surgery would affect me when I returned to school. I did have to become more guarded as I walked through the busy hallways to class. If someone accidentally stepped on my foot or I banged it into something, I would literally be in a temporary world of pain to the point of tears, although it would quickly subside. This didn't stop me from wrestling though.

I had been on the wrestling team since I had been a freshman. I became an excellent wrestler, winning almost all of my matches. In the fall of 1971, my senior year in high school, I was on the varsity wrestling team participating in the ninety-eight pound weight class. I was very proud of my athletic prowess and worried about how my damaged right foot would affect my performance.

The pride I felt from my wrestling achievements and the respect that they had helped me gain from my fellow classmates meant a lot to me. I remember experiencing the greatest joy when Martha, a friend in my physics class, asked me to speak to her brother. He was a freshman that year and she wanted me to speak to him about joining the wrestling team. She knew I was into the sport since I spoke about it often and Martha had also seen me in action, winning my matches during various school tournaments. I guess she was impressed with my wrestling performances, since she asked me to talk to her brother. When I first joined the wrestling team I had only weighed seventy-five pounds. During my senior year I was only five feet six and weighed barely ninety-eight pounds.

Anyway, Martha felt that being on the wrestling team would help her brother develop character since he was built on the small side, as I was. I waited to meet him one day in the school courtyard. Standing by the drinking fountain, I waited as this blond-headed kid came sauntering over, walking as if he owned the world. I told him how wrestling would make him tougher than any other sport he could think of or decide to try. I explained how it would give him an opportunity to go up against someone in his size and weight class. I described how it would give him an even chance of excelling in a sport.

Martha's brother tapped his foot, his eyes looking around the schoolyard as I compared the virtues of wrestling to football and basketball. Finally his patience ended. "Listen, he said, the kid in my weight class is tough as hell. No one in the school can beat him. I'll never get the varsity spot, so why should I even try."

Suppressing a smile, I told him he should still try out and spend his first year learning the sport and preparing to be the best in his weight class the following year or even the year after. He said no thanks and took off. As he rounded the corner, I let the laughter escape my lips as my chest swelled with pride. I was the kid in his weight class who no one in the whole school could beat. I loved wrestling so much! It gave me, the slightly built kid that I was, the edge I needed to excel in a sport. My teammates and I did so well that we were all invited to attend a state regional wrestling tournament.

I have always demanded respect from others and although I was small in size, I was very large in spirit. I always felt just as important as all the big guys in the school did. I never let my size diminish my spirit, or prevent me from being accepted as an absolute equal. From time to time my attitude most definitely got me in trouble with kids who were bigger than me. Some big kids turned out to be big jerks. My grandfather, Alan, would always have something to say to me when I would tell him about an incident in school relating to my size. When he would see me seriously depressed about this size issue, he would just say, "Remember a dime is smaller than a penny, but it's ten times more valuable, and don't you ever forget that."

Wrestling season always started at the tail end of football season. Usually I eagerly anticipated the start of the season, however this year I was nervous. We would all line up, strip down and get weighed so the coaches could verify the weight class to which we belonged. My stomach turned over and I thought I would throw up as I took my socks and shoes off and prepared to join the other boys by the scale. Undressed, I marched over to the scale. As I stood on the cold weight scale, my scarred right foot, with its missing toe, was exposed for everyone to see. I was sure everyone was staring at my right foot. I was relieved when no one mentioned a word about my foot and I wondered if anyone noticed. I wrestled well that season, winning most of my matches, and was rewarded with a letter jacket after the season ended. I treasured that jacket and still have it in a special place in my closet.

The regional tournament in Carlsbad, New Mexico, was one of the most interesting and challenging events in my wrestling career. I walked into what was the largest single room I had ever been in for a wrestling tournament. There were at least eight wrestling mats covering the floor, with vivid splashes of color. Some mats were purple with light blue delineating the out-of-bounds area and the center point of the match area. Other mats were dark brown with white trim, orange highlighted with blue, and yellow edged with green. Our school had a match against a high school for the blind, so each person on our team had to wrestle a blind kid in our respective weight class. I watched the kids from the blind school warming up. As I watched, I noticed them apparently unconcerned about what people thought about their disability. I felt pathetic and ashamed. I was so concerned about what people thought about me, seeing my foot with an amputated toe. How could I be so damn self-conscious about it when all those blind kids were ready to wrestle and win for themselves and their school? I quickly found myself feeling profound respect and admiration for those tough blind kids. I saw them as being very brave souls, braver than I was. Our coach cautioned us not to feel sorry for our opponents because they were blind. "Remember, your opponent won't feel sorry for you!" I couldn't feel sorry for my opponent because he was winning every match. He won the regional tournament in our weight class. However, it turned out that I was the only one he couldn't pin. That gave me a bit of pride in myself and respect from my teammates, although my coach was still obviously very pissed off at me all afternoon. You see I always had more pressure put on me by the coach because the lowest weight class always went first in a team wrestling match. If you won that first match, that was a fantastic thing for team spirit. If you lost, well I won't say how I felt or the team felt about that, you can imagine. It was an honor to be in the ninety-eight pound weight class and I always truly believed that and worked very hard to be the best wrestler I could. That match with the blind kid was more important than many that I had won. It taught me that I would be okay, despite the loss of my toe. Whatever I had to face was better than being blind. If he could make something of himself even though he was blind, I would do fine even with only nine toes.

School and wrestling were interrupted by periodic checkups. The doctors had found cancer after they studied the growth that they had completely removed from my foot. It turned out that the tumor began developing at the bottom of the inside of my foot. The doctors thought that the tumor had begun growing in the bottom of my foot and then formed a tube that took a path to my toe bone and began attacking it. They believed that the increased blood flow to the broken toe attracted the tumor and encouraged it to grow there. The tumor dissolved bone tissue, creating a cavity in the bone as it continued to grow up and around the surface of my foot. It surrounded the other foot bones like the Blob from the old Steve McQueen movie. It had spread under the skin until it pushed the skin up, creating the bump. I found the whole story very hard to believe. It didn't make any sense to me. I thought that it was only an educated guess, at best. They really couldn't know for sure! Every three months my mom and I had to make a trip to Houston. This is how the doctors could make sure that no tumors were growing and that every last cancerous cell was excised from my body. For the next ten years, I would have to undergo periodic examinations before I could be declared cancer free and know for sure that other than missing a toe, my right foot was just fine.

Chapter 4

Follow-up Appointments

By the third follow-up visit I had become accustomed to the routine. Mom and I would travel to Houston and then go directly to the hospital where we would wait in a huge room with dozens of other patients. We had learned that the surgeons operated in the morning and reserved the afternoon for consultations and follow-up visits. The doctors would have all their patients come in at 1:00 P.M. and sit around and wait until they were called.

That May afternoon, Mom and I were back in Houston for the third follow-up visit. We sat in the brightly lit waiting room, which was, as always, filled to capacity with patients and family members. I thought the dark green marble floor tiles made the giant room seem classier than a hospital clinic. The interminable wait made me jumpy and unsettled. I didn't want to be part of this sea of humanity, waiting for the all clear to keep the rest of my body intact.

My impatience made it impossible for me to concentrate on schoolwork or other diversions that needed deliberate attention. Reading got old fast. The contents of the magazines bored me. The light reflecting off the glossy pages annoyed me. Reading had never been one of my favorite activities and trying to absorb what was on the pages under those circumstances nauseated me.

Instead, I found different ways to entertain myself. One of my favorite diversions was to bother my mother. I would think of things to do and say that I was sure would evoke a reaction. My favorite one was to say, " Let's go! I can't take this sitting around any more!" Mom would just smile and continue to read her magazine. She never even glanced up when I said that. Even though my antics elicited very little reaction from Mom, I still found it extremely entertaining. I had her all to myself. I didn't have to share her with my brothers. It was just Mom and me, and I liked that attention very much. She was mine alone to bother and I enjoyed that a lot. I guess dealing with me was more frustrating and boring than trying to read her magazine in glaring light. It was surely more interesting than my inane questions.

People watching provided the most entertainment. I would look around the room and wonder why all these people were here. I was probably better off not knowing their stories since from time to time we heard about some very sad situations. Sometimes just looking around at the mangled people sitting in row after row of perfectly aligned silver-framed and black vinyl chairs was just too much. This time there was a beautiful young lady sitting across the aisle from me. She had long, straight, shiny brown hair, big brown eyes, a slender face and an ivory complexion. She sat with her back straight and her head held high with pride. Her posture had an almost regal bearing to it. She was wearing a poncho that completely covered her upper body. Slowly I realized that she must have selected that garment because she wanted to conceal the fact that she only had one arm.

The girl was in good shape compared to the man occupying the chair at the end of my row. His lower jaw had been completely removed. A white gauze pad that was drenched with his spittle was hanging out of his mouth. It had been placed there in an attempt to prevent his saliva from dripping out of what remained of his mouth and soaking him. I knew I shouldn't, but I couldn't help staring at him. Eventually he looked back at me, and I looked away. I could not comprehend that he was a man looking back at me, a fellow human being, not some alien from another universe. It was unbelievable that a human could look the way he did. When I allowed myself to finally accept that this was a guy that just had his lower jaw removed, feelings of sadness overwhelmed me so quickly and so deeply that I had to distract myself and think of something else quickly or I would have probably started crying.

During this visit we had to wait until 6:00 P.M. before the doctor could see us. I lost track of how many times I had told my mother I was ready to leave. Dr. Edmend was new to my case. He was overweight, short, and balding. His beady eyes needed thick glasses to help them see my thick chart and x-rays. He droned on about the state of my condition, saying that the chest x-ray and blood work-up was fine. He spoke mainly to my mom. My thoughts drifted off as I wondered if I could ask to borrow his glasses. They were so thick that I was sure that I could quickly start a fire using the lenses and the sun next time I went camping with my friends. Yep, those glasses, hot sun, and a dry dark gray piece of old Mesquite wood would start a great fire.

This is what I was thinking as a disturbing comment pricked through my daydream. Dr. Edmend said that if they had realized any cancer was present prior to the surgery that removed my toe, they would have removed half of my foot at the same time instead of just my toe. "That's the only way to be sure that no growth will reoccur in the future," he said. That's great, I thought, I could have lost half of my foot instead of just one toe. I was very happy that things had worked out as they had. It was tough enough dealing with a missing toe. I didn't want to think how it would be to walk around with only half a foot. Mom paled after hearing the doctor's remarks. I was shaken up, but I just wanted to get out of the hospital and back to El Paso. I was ready to get on with my life. I thought the worst was over. I will be fine, I thought. This crap is over. I'm fine. Let's go!

19

Chapter 5

Houston, Here I Come Solo

The next follow-up visit was scheduled for April, about a year after the surgery that took my toe. I felt that my foot looked fine. I would study its appearance from time to time, examining it from every possible angle. Although I noticed that some swelling developed on the top of my foot over the old surgery area, I rationalized that it was just scar tissue that had formed over the past year. As far as I was concerned, my foot looked fine, I felt fine, and these follow-up visits were a waste of time and money. Going to Houston for my regular checkups was about as eventful as yearly visits to the dentist. No cavities, not a problem with my foot.

By now I had so much experience going to these regular appointments that my parents decided I could go alone. I looked forward to traveling by myself and feeling independent. Things were tight financially for my parents and not having to spend money on Mom's airfare would definitely be beneficial. My cousins, Judy and Max, who lived in a nice suburb in the Houston area with their four young boys, Josh, Allen, Bill and Joey, were available to pick me up at the airport and take me to the hospital for my appointment. Everything had become so routine, so even my overly protective mother felt at ease with the notion of me making this visit without her.

The plane ride was uneventful. I had fantasized that my seatmate would be an absolutely gorgeous babe who would find me undeniably attractive and we would be madly in love by the time the plane landed in Houston. Instead of finding an alluring blond looking up at me with adoring blue eyes, the person occupying the seat next to mine was an obese elderly lady whose sour expression seemed to declare that she was pissed off at the world. Her bulk rolled into my seat as she put her plump arm firmly over the shared armrest. I looked out the window the entire flight, enjoying the view of the clouds and fields below, daydreaming and enjoying my independence, even though I was a little lonely. When the plane landed, I sauntered off in what I had hoped was a cool, independent manner, as I was met by my cousins and their entire family.

The next day I confidently went for what I was sure would be a routine exam. The exam room was small, almost claustrophobic. A bright white light illuminated the room, which had blue cabinets on all the walls and an exam table in the middle. The harsh mixture of antiseptics and other medicines tickled my nose. Suddenly the door opened and a doctor finally came in. I had never met this doctor, but he seemed nervous. My hair stood on end, but I had no idea how his words were going to change my life. He introduced himself as Dr. Doomalson, a resident doctor who had been asked to perform my evaluation for the exam. He scanned my chart, then looked at me and asked if he could examine my right foot. He held my cold foot in his warm hand and began to lightly push and squeeze the area that had been operated on, near the toes but on the top of the foot, close to my big toe. He abruptly stood up and announced that he would return in a few minutes. When he re-entered the room, Dr. Doomalson was accompanied by five other doctors, all clad in white lab coats and wearing serious expressions. I felt my blood pressure rising.

They all crowded into the room and focused on my foot. One of them pressed firmly on the top of the surgery area, another squished the sides of the wounded area. Another just had a solemn expression, but said nothing. All the doctors were serious and eager to see my foot. All of them were deep in thought, apparently fascinated by the overall appearance of my foot. They did not include me as

21

they discussed my foot in cryptic medical jargon. After about four or five long minutes they left. The door closed and I was left alone to contemplate their strange behavior.

After a while, Dr. Doomalson returned and took the same seat he had when he first began my exam. He didn't look calm and nonchalant. He looked concerned and upset. His voice quivered as he asked, "How old are you?" Why would he be nervous about asking me how old I was? This visit was no longer routine. "I'm seventeen," I answered. His eyes dropped to the floor as though it pained him to look directly at me. He slowly lifted his head as though it had doubled in weight, and looked me right in the eyes. He asked if there was anyone with me. I told him that my cousins were picking me up after the appointment, but there was no one with me at the hospital. He hesitated before he blurted out the shocking news. "We feel you have a ninety-five percent chance of having your right foot amputated due to the reoccurrence of the tumor," he said. I was quiet for some very long seconds. Tears welled at the corners of my eyes. The pit of my stomach tightened, and I almost shook with emotion. I just wanted to leave that exam room. Surely if I just left, everything would go back to normal. Those horrible words with their gruesome image would go away, if only I could get out of the hospital. I just wanted to leave, I thought, as the panicked feeling grew worse. I'm not dealing with this. I'm not going to come back to this hospital, I thought as I started feeling more in control.

Dr. Doomalson looked at me with concern, trying to decide how I was accepting his news. "Don't think of not coming back here," he said. I hadn't realized that mind reading was one of his talents. "The tumor will continue to grow until it begins to stretch your skin and eventually it will try to break through your skin. It must be removed from your body." I didn't respond. I didn't blink or say a word. Again, he said, "The tumor must be removed."

"You said ninety-five percent. What does that mean exactly?" I asked after I was finally able to organize my thoughts.

"We will test the tumor for cancer. There is a possibility that we could leave you with part of your foot if there is no cancer present, but we really don't recommend it. Going through life at your age with part of a foot can lead to arthritis in the remaining ankle joint, giving you a painful ankle that's of little use to you. I conferred with my colleagues and we all feel it is cancerous and the best thing for you to do at this time would be to have the foot removed just above the ankle so you are rid of the tumor," he explained. He looked at me to see if I understood what he was telling me. "We would then test the remaining tissue and bone at the bottom of your leg to make sure all the cancer is gone before we finish the surgery and stitch you up. We feel the tumor is growing slowly enough for you to go back home and finish high school and return for the surgery in three months. You should have a very successful outcome," he said.

I told him that my brother was having his Bar Mitzvah in June and I asked if it would be okay if I had the surgery after that. The doctor said the tumor was growing slowly enough and the three month wait would be fine. "Tomorrow we will need to do some lab workups to check on a few more things before you return home," he said. He left the room and I followed along behind him like a puppy. He showed me where to go for the lab work and said goodbye. I felt so alone. I was the saddest I had ever been in my entire life. I found a phone and called my cousin, Max, to tell him that my appointment was finished and I was ready to be picked up. I could not get the words out fast enough. I started crying, telling him that I had a ninety-five percent chance of losing my entire foot. I hadn't meant to tell him that news over the phone, but I needed to tell someone and the words just poured out. Max must have flown to get to the hospital as he arrived so quickly. It seemed as if I had just hung up the phone and there he was. I was happy as hell to see him. We went back to his house and as soon as we arrived, I asked to call my mother and father.

It was a terrible call to my mother. The emotions of the call cloud my recollection of the details. My mother answered the phone with her normal worrisome, concerned motherly personality. I knew this news would distress her, but I needed to share this tragic news with her and my father. First, I told her everything the doctor had told me. She wept quietly and gave the phone to my dad, who tried very hard to accept what I was telling him without revealing any emotion over the phone. He could not hide what he was feeling, and his voice choked until he couldn't speak anymore. He handed the phone back to my mom. She had used those few minutes to compose herself, but her voice still shook. "I want to know everything, so tell me it to me again," she said. In dull monotone, I repeated the doctor's news with its tragic and unbelievable consequences. She asked when I would be coming home and I told her that I had to take some tests the next day before coming home. She asked to speak to my cousin, Max. He assured her he would not leave my side until I was on the plane home. Mom asked me to pray and ask for God's help with this situation. I said I would and I hung up the phone and moved away from it. I felt like a Zombie with no place to go. I desperately wanted to find peace.

My cousin, Max, was sensitive to my situation. He asked if I wanted to talk and stayed quiet when I didn't. Max was very good to me. His behavior and kindness surprised me since he was usually so serious and distracted all the time. He insisted on staying with me all day in the hospital. I don't know if he did it because my mom asked him to or his wife, Judy, told him to, but I needed and appreciated his

24

company. He was a busy real estate agent so I knew it was a sacrifice for him to take a whole day to be with me. I have never forgotten that act of kindness by my cousin, Max, and have always remembered him and his whole family for their benevolent help throughout my ordeal.

The first thing the doctors did was draw blood. They ordered the phlebotomist to take a huge syringe full, so much that I almost fainted. They gave me some orange juice and made me rest for a few minutes before I went for a chest x-ray. I had to stay in Houston for one more day while they studied the results and decided if more tests were necessary. I was glad when I received permission to go home. The surgery was set for June 22, 1971. I didn't want to think about what would happen on that day.

Looking at the clouds as the plane carried me home, I debated what type of front I wanted to present to my friends and family. Surely, I could milk this horrid situation for all that it was worth. I could receive tons of sympathy and have everyone wait on me hand and foot or I could be a tough guy and act like nothing bothered me. After much contemplation, I decided to be the tough guy, and deny myself the luxury of expressing my true, legitimate feelings. I wasn't going to show my overwhelming anger at finding myself in this horrendous situation. I wasn't sure how to adjust to this. I didn't have the ability to adjust. I would be the macho, tough guy. No one would see me exhibit any feelings. I found myself trapped in a state of non-accepting limbo. It was my newly discovered destiny to become a foot amputee. I wasn't sure how I would deal with it.

Getting ready to land in El Paso was such a strange sight. The desert looked as if some giant alien vacuum device just sucked up everything green with some color-sucking contraption. All you could see from the plane were a million shades of brown, from the lightest barely tan to the darkest almost black. There was a strange beauty to it, I thought, as the expanse of it was pierced through the middle by the Franklin Mountain Range with its winding jagged peaks and valleys, and beautiful sunset out in the distance. I looked to the west. The desert seemed to stretch on forever over the mesas of the lower valley where it finally reached out to the beautiful, colorful sun-setting sky. The magnificent multi-colored sky consisted of light blues, pinks, oranges and brilliant shades of purple. The plane finally landed and I emerged into the welcoming embrace of my family.

Chapter 6

Dreading Going Back to School

No one in the family seemed to know what to do or say. My mom and dad and my brothers were very quiet and let me do whatever I wanted with little interference. There was a cloud of sadness surrounding our family. It was almost as if someone had died, and I couldn't ignore the fact that I was the one responsible for generating that atmosphere. My older brother, Ed, who was two years my senior had no idea how he could help me deal with the inner turmoil I was feeling. He didn't seem to realize that I might need his help. I didn't resent that, because I hadn't realized that I could have used his help either. Eric, my younger brother, was just twelve at the time and he didn't have a clue about what I was thinking or feeling.

When I went out with my friends I could forget about the pending surgery. My friends were a great distraction. Everyone had something to do, someplace to go and there was just plain fun to be had. I found myself going out with my friends at every opportunity. I wanted to thoroughly enjoy these last carefree, whole-body days. I didn't want the last three months of my senior year to focus solely on my upcoming operation. I didn't want to think about what was going to happen to me when school ended, and that would only be possible if no one at high school was aware of my impending ordeal. Unfortunately that was not meant to be.

My mom obviously had a different approach to dealing with the stress she had endured from my medical situation. She wanted to talk. One of the people she chose to share with was my friend, Andy's, mom. My mom told Andy's mom all the details of the amputation of my foot scheduled for June. Andy's mom told him all about it and he made sure that the news spread. Needless to say, the whole student body began wondering why I was back. Why was I not having surgery, and what exactly was going on with my foot? Walking down the hall, people would stop and stare. I felt like my foot had a big arrow on it, drawing everyone's attention to it. I was very angry that I was such a great topic of discussion. I really thought that I could keep the whole thing a secret and that no one would ever know; you see that was my plan! I thought I could graduate high school and no one would know what I would be doing over the summer because school would be over. I would tell whomever I wanted to in my own good time, when I felt ready to share my most personal situation with a select few of my closest friends. I just wanted to keep it a secret.

I was glad that most of my friends would be scattering when school was finished. They were going all over the country to different colleges, and some of them were even going to travel for a few months before starting college. This would all work in my favor, I thought. No one would be around, everyone would be off doing his or her own thing, and no one would focus on me.

I was so pissed off at Andy for spreading the rumor about my most personal situation. Well, I guess it wasn't a rumor, since I was going to have surgery in June, but it was my story and I hadn't wanted it circulating throughout the school. Naturally, he denied telling anyone. Even though he swore that he hadn't said anything to anyone, I never believed him. I vowed to get even with him some day soon. I felt like really smacking him around. I did eventually confront him. I found myself yelling at him, our faces less than an inch apart, my face filled with rage, his with fear. I thought his eyes would pop out of his head! I felt deeply violated by my so-called friend, Andy. I had known him almost since the first day we moved to El Paso when I was just ten years old and we used to spend a lot of time together. In high school we weren't as friendly as we had been when we were younger. I knew he was a storyteller because he told them all the time, but I never knew he could be so insensitive. I guess he just couldn't resist a good hot story no matter whose feelings got hurt in the process. We weren't close anymore, but I didn't think he would deliberately make me an object of his gossip. As much as I could, I downplayed all the comments, ignored the questions, and disregarded the strange and pitying looks that I received. Relatively soon the buzz at school had calmed down and I was very grateful for that. It was enough to deal with the fact that in three months, on June 22, 1971, I would be having my right foot amputated. I didn't need a constant reminder of it from anyone. I would deal with it in my own way!

I was very stoic and my father observed, "You seem to be handling this situation very well. It doesn't seem to bother you at all." "There is nothing I can do about it, so why worry or go around being upset about it?" I said. However, I thought about it every damn day, although I would never actually allow myself to dwell on the details of what was going on and what would be happening all too soon. If I let myself think about what I would undergo in June, I would probably have cried every day. I was also concealing an immense amount of anger and resentment. I kept thinking, "Why me; what did I do to deserve this? What have I done in the past that was so terrible that I deserved this punishment?"

Sometimes I would actually have the luxury of forgetting about it for short periods of time as I went about living my life as best as I could, trying to forget about what was about to happen. I would look at my right foot some nights before going to sleep and actually find myself talking to my foot as if it wasn't part of my body. "You're going to be gone soon," I'd say to my right foot. It looked fine; it felt fine. Why did it have to go? Some nights I would stare at the foot, almost willing it to answer. I hated this nonstop

29

nightmare in which I found myself. Most nights I would lie in bed, praying for help. Often I couldn't sleep, but would toss and turn, sometimes burying my face in the pillow, wanting to scream; other times staring up into the blackness, asking for help, hoping that I would come out of this nightmare intact.

I still have the last picture of myself with my right foot. I was wearing a bathing suit and standing in our driveway next to the black 1968 Volkswagen Beetle that my older brother and I shared. We were so proud of that car. Most of our friends didn't have one. This was our car to share; my dad had given it to us because we would both be needing it for college soon and with Mom and Dad working all the time, we really needed it to get around town. My brother, Ed, and I took turns driving it on the weekends up until I wrecked it, which wasn't all that long after we got it. I felt sick about the $475.00 worth of damage that occurred and that used up all my savings. The car had been a great diversion and helped keep my mind off the impending surgery. I was just starting to go on dates and have fun with my friends, and having a car made this easier and so much more fun.

We were having one of the best times together when the car accident happened. I had been sharing a mini-six-pack of beer with a friend, Johnny, and our girlfriends, April and Saundra. We were all under twenty-one and disregarding the legal drinking age in the state of Texas. But we were partying, having fun, and didn't really care that according to the Texas state legislature, you had to be twenty-one to drink. As we consumed those beers, we loosened up considerably on that starlit night parked on the Rio Grande levee. On the way back to the party, my girlfriend, Saundra, put her head in my lap as she lay on her back across the front seat as I drove. She put her arms around my neck. "Kiss me," she implored with a drunken sexy pout of her lips. She was definitely feeling the effects of the beer. I had a little sense left in me and I shook my head. "Please," she said pulling my head down and looking all too tempting. I then decided that I was talented enough to continue driving and kiss her at the same time. I had rationalized that if I drove slowly enough I could hold the steering wheel straight and the car would just go straight down the road through the neighborhood. No problem I thought; this way we could get back to the party without too much delay and we could be kissing a little. As our make-out session intensified, the car angled slightly off the road and suddenly we found ourselves shooting through a small irrigation canal that acted like a ramp, shooting us up into the air clipping off the top of a stone wall. I saw a tree bounce off the hood of the car with an eardrum shattering crash. It hit the top of the car, bouncing a couple of times before it rolled over my beautiful black 1968 Beetle and fell to the side as the car finally stopped with a crunch.

Physically we were okay. My girlfriend tore the skin around her pierced ear a little bit. No one else suffered even minor wounds. Mentally is another story. I was stressed to the max already and with my dad having to come and get me, I just felt terrible. While dealing with the police that were called by the homeowners whose property I had just damaged, I thought I would have a heart attack any minute and pass out. Suddenly the nighttime blackness of the upper valley in the desert city of El Paso looked much darker and felt much colder, as I was truly about to pass out. Driving home with my dad, all I could think about was how horribly my life was going and wondered how I would survive everything. When Dad and I arrived home, he said only four words to me: "You're paying for everything!" My dad had always been strict. I didn't think of asking him to help me pay for it, or asking him to take pity on me because of what I was going through. When he spoke only four words and said nothing else, I knew I had gotten off easy. All I had to do was pay for all the damages I had caused. I wasn't grounded at all. I think my dad didn't punish me strongly because he knew I was going through a most difficult time in my life. I thought Ed would kill me when I told him about it, but he quickly calmed down. He even thought the story about how the accident had occurred was kind of funny. I wasn't laughing! I think Ed went easy on me too.

My friend, Johnny, and his girlfriend were very upset about it all and stayed that way for weeks. The accident took place about a month before my surgery and I barely spoke to my friend again until well after the surgery. My girlfriend had to deal with the fact that I blamed her for the whole thing. I wound up never speaking to her again after the accident. It was also my last date for a long time, not because of anybody else, just me.

The house my car landed in belonged to Margaret in my physics class. I was surprised to learn this the next school day. I pleaded with her to have her father go easy on me as he figured out all the damages to their property and prepared a bill for me to pay. I begged her all through the class period. She was very nice, surprisingly so, and assured me that she would do her best to convince her father to give me a break. He ended up just sending me copies of all the repair costs and had me reimburse him. Somehow I managed to pay him back. As I washed pots and pans in a local cafeteria, I regretted that my wages went to Margaret's father, rather than into my own pocket. Over very hot soapy water, I vowed never to get so drunk that I let alcohol make me so stupid.

Finally, graduation day arrived and along with the rest of the class of 1971, I left Coronado High School behind me. I was thrilled that four long boring years of high school were finally completed. There was a sense of finality and a feeling of accomplishment. Graduating was something I had looked forward to from the first day I set foot in the high school building. However, I had no idea that I would have such mixed feelings about graduation once the day finally arrived. Graduation meant that the upcoming surgery was just around the corner and I had been making great efforts not to think about it at all. The distraction of school was now over.

When Grandma Ida and Grandpa Joe came to town, I started feeling even more uneasy. They didn't make me feel uncomfortable, but their arrival was another signal that the clock was ticking down until it would be time for surgery. They insisted on driving Mom and me from El Paso to the hospital in Houston and staying for a few days after the surgery. Jacob, my grandfather's brother, and his wife, Penina, came from Israel for my brother, Eric's, Bar Mitzvah and stayed for my surgery. Dad didn't come with us to Houston since he had to stay home and work and also manage my two brothers, well mainly my younger brother, the Bar Mitzvah boy.

Soon we left for Houston in my grandfather's gorgeous, huge, metallic greenish-silver Buick Electra 225 Wildcat, with a light green plush interior and excellent air conditioning. My grandmother took the greatest pride in telling everyone, with her heavy Russian accent, that she would have to put her sweater on in the car at times because the A/C was so powerful and the car would get too cold. I got to sit up front next to the driver, my grandfather, and my grandmother, the aggravating co-pilot. They loved me so much I could always really feel it when I was with them, and I liked that very much. We drove for a long time before we finally stopped for an overnight stay at some hotel that I'm sure was highly recommended by the AAA organization to which my grandfather subscribed. He had designed our road map and we followed it meticulously. The road map was affectionately called a "Trip Ticket" by Grandpa. I was getting some exercise out in the parking lot of the motel, walking around on these brick walls, testing my great balancing skills and just enjoying stretching my legs when my mom strolled over and asked me, "What are you doing?" I thought for a second before I replied, "I might as well enjoy my balancing skills now because I will never be able to do this again." Her look of curiosity was replaced by one of sadness. Of course what I said freaked Mom out very much. She had nothing else to say and she promptly walked away, leaving me alone with my angry attitude. My poor mom; I don't know how she put up with me throughout this most terrible time in my life.

I really didn't sleep much at all that night as I was so jumpy inside. I was agitated down to my innermost core. It was a long drive east to Houston, but we finally got there the next day. It was amazing to be driving for a whole day and still be in the same state. Texas is truly a great big beautiful state. I think the most annoying thing about the drive was dealing with the alarm buzzer that my grandfather would set so he wouldn't drive over the speed limit. On the linear speedometer in the dash there was this needle with a little bright red ball on it that could be moved to the speed number you wanted to drive under by turning a little dial. If you passed it because you were driving too fast, you were forced to hear an annoying electric buzzing sound until you slowed to under that specific speed. Well it buzzed all across the huge state of Texas making it seem even bigger if that's possible. I had buzzing in my ears well after we arrived in Houston and were freed from the confines of the car. I was feeling even more nervous now probably because of that damn awful buzzing noise.

Chapter 7

June 22, 1971

The time before the surgery was just a blur. The intensity of that time was so powerful that I was numbed into a protective mental cocoon that sheltered me so that I could survive what was to come. I just could not think about it any more. If I did, I would have just died of fright. It was in that state of mind that I was wheeled into surgery again.

When I woke up this time, things were more serious than ever before. Gazing down at my leg, I could tell that it no longer ended in a foot. Eventually, I peeked under the thin white sheet and saw a white gauze bandage wrapped in the form of a small volleyball around my right ankle area. I looked down my leg to see what they had done to me. Under the thin white sheet glowing from the fluorescent brilliant white light I could see that there was obviously no foot there any longer!

I did not realize until approximately ten years later how deep a state of denial I had put myself in. Apparently in order for me to emotionally survive the loss of my foot I had to deny my true feelings. I did discover these feelings at a later time in my life as I carried them deep inside me for years like unclaimed baggage just waiting patiently for the right moment to be unpacked and put away forever clearing my innocent mind. It would have been healthier if I had been able to express them outwardly and openly right then, once I knew and actually saw that my right foot was removed from my body permanently. Instead, seconds later a pain ignited in my lower leg and traveled to my brain like an ultra-fast railroad locomotive. Agitated and upset, I called out for help. They gave me something that eventually helped ease the pain. Dr. Green had left orders for pain medication to be administered every four hours. However, the medication only worked for three hours, so I suffered for one very long agonizing hour after every shot wore off. That first night was the worst.

When the doctor came to check on me the next morning, I complained about my painful suffering situation. He adjusted the amount of medication I was given and it became easier to deal with the pain. The next three days were still a living hell of pain. While the enhanced pain medication helped, I was extremely sensitive to movement, anyone's movement. The slightest vibration from anyone walking into the room, especially near my bed, caused waves of pain to start up and move in an undulating manner up and down my leg and explode in my brain. I had to lie perfectly still, almost frozen, in order to minimize the pain when I was conscious. The pain was so absolutely horrible that when I saw the nurse coming with my injection, I flipped the sheets down and in one second, had my underpants lowered with my hip exposed. I was ready for the shot that I so desperately needed. I had rows of puncture marks from all the shots I was receiving so that my hips began to look like a connect-the-dots picture.

When I was awake, the worst thing anyone could do to me was touch the bed. One time, my Uncle Jack walked in the room to visit and I yelled at him to stop walking! His jaw dropped as he had never heard me yell like that, but he graciously obeyed, and like an awkward dancer he stopped in his tracks with a half twirl. He looked at my mom with question and concern in his eyes before he put the gift he had bought me on the bedside table and slowly moved away. Uncle Jack had traveled down from New Jersey to see me and have a little vacation at the same time. I appreciated that he wanted to come to see me. I couldn't enjoy his visit during those first few days in the hospital. I really didn't want to see anyone. Everyone learned to move gingerly around the bed. Eventually I recovered my manners enough to thank Uncle Jack for the big portable radio he had brought me.

My grandfather was deeply affected by all that had happened to me. He was remarkably compassionate as he tried to do anything he could think of to ease my discomfort. I had been a big T.V. addict, so he paid to have a T.V. brought in for me to watch. He knew things were bad when I had no desire to watch the T.V. and was in too much distress to watch any of my favorite programs.

I finally began to feel better after the first couple of nights, when the strangest thing happened. While I was sleeping on my stomach I noticed that I would find myself pulling myself upwards towards the head of the bed. I did this because I didn't feel my right foot on the surface of the sheets and thought it was hanging over the edge. I would keep pulling myself up the bed. This only happened during the twilight of my sleep, or Twilight Zone of my sleep, is more like it. Just as strange were the aptly named phantom pains that began to develop. I mostly felt the strange sensation of my little toe flexing and straightening and hurting in the motion process as if it was being squeezed at the same time. I guess my brain was trying to become accustomed to the idea that the foot was no longer attached to my body. This process didn't stop for a long while; it only became less intense.

To my happy surprise this hospital surgical visit was very short. After ten days they took the stitches out of my perfectly performed Syme type amputation. Dr. Green told me that not such a long time ago, Dr. Syme had discovered a way to remove a foot from one's leg in such a precise way as to leave the heel skin intact so one could actually stand on the amputated limb comfortably. He created a kind of real flesh and blood peg leg that could actually be walked on. Of course, one leg then became about three inches shorter than the other but this ingenious surgical technique allowed you

37

to walk and stand unassisted for short periods of time. You could then do important things that we all take for granted, like take a shower and make nightly visits to the bathroom. Just standing unassisted or balancing on your own without crutches was very helpful. I was really just thinking to myself that I was separated finally from the strange destructive tumor that invaded my healthy body and attacked me, ruining my foot and my life. After giving me a brief, but well appreciated education on the Syme amputation technique, Dr. Green informed me that the vicious tumor I had had was called an "Osteo type Desmoid Tumor Grade III."

My next follow-up appointment was set for three months later. At that time he would check to make sure that the remaining limb was stable and well healed from the surgery. He cautioned me not to walk or put any weight bearing pressure on it until the limb was well healed and he authorized me to do so.

Before I left, I asked him a question that had been on my mind for some time now, "Would I ever have cancer again at any other time in my life?" Without hesitating, he replied, "You have a nine percent chance of some type of reoccurrence at some time in your life." I thought about that for a while and eventually rationalized that those were damn good odds and I was damn lucky. I remembered hearing that most people have a twenty-five percent chance of getting some type of cancer at some time in their life. I thought that I got off easy especially compared to other people I had seen and learned about during my time at M.D. Anderson. It was truly a great, life-saving hospital! I saw the reality of the true saying, "It can always be worse!" Actually the other patients secretly helped me get through my trauma. They, who suffered through worse things than I had, had enabled me to see how lucky I was to still have my life. I knew I could get by somehow and it all became a bit easier to cope with. I was finally starting to have some positive thoughts, and that felt good, but it didn't last too long.

My grandparents had driven back to Cleveland after they saw that I was improving. They felt comfortable leaving Mom and me a few days after the surgery and left with my aunt and uncle from Israel. Grandpa Joe and Bubbie Ida were always very caring and loving grandparents and I have always been truly blessed to have them as my grandparents and be a large part of my life.

Mom and I arrived at the airport in El Paso and were greeted by my brothers and dad. As we entered the airport terminal, Dad took one look at me as I walked along on my crutches and quickly turned away. He began crying uncontrollably and it made me feel worse than I already did. I guess that even though he had known what the results of my surgery would be, he wasn't ready to deal with seeing the reality of it all. I really felt physically sick in the pit of my stomach at this time. It was strange seeing people in the airport looking at me with question in their eyes. I knew they were probably wondering what had happened to this unfortunate kid as they saw the obvious emotional wrecks who were my family. The toughest thing was seeing my dad cry. I just couldn't deal with it, but somehow I found the strength to just keep moving along like an emotionless robot. I just kept traveling along on my crutches in the little El Paso airport all the while feeling an overwhelming sadness about the reality of my new life as an amputee and seeing it unfold in front of me in real time. The huge windows in the hallway allowed welcomed natural light in which bathed over us as we slowly went to collect our luggage and then to our red Ford station wagon.

My brothers had no idea what to say to me. There was an awkward silence in the car. They tried to make some small talk and joke around about stuff. I wasn't laughing. I appreciated their efforts, but I was really hurting inside and my mood was pretty fixed and didn't budge as they could easily see. We finally got home and I went directly to my familiar perfect, peaceful and private bedroom that I now really appreciated in a new and different way. I spent a lot of time in this quiet haven over the next three months, actually way too much time, hiding myself away from the world.

Chapter 8

Convalescing in my Bedroom

When I was settled in my room I found a nice surprise. Sitting on the table next to my bed was a brand new black and white television that my dad's poker playing buddies had bought for me. My first cousins and other extended family in Cleveland, Ohio, had sent gifts and cards with nice words of concern to the house. Stewart and Eleanor especially and even their little sister Jenna seemed to have taken it all pretty badly. Later I found out more details from my mom. Stewart, Eleanor, Jenna and I shared Grandpa Alan and Grandma Della, as our mothers were sisters. Their mom, my Aunt Ruth, was very concerned about me. I think she was even more of a worrier than my mom. She always sent us, my brothers and me, birthday cards and gifts as she is a good caring aunt and has always wanted to maintain a close relationship with all of us. We moved to El Paso from Cleveland when I was ten years old and my cousins used to spend a lot of time with my brothers and me during those ten years. We had become quite close during that time.

My next-door neighbor, Albert, was my best friend in El Paso. His parents came over to tell me that they kept their son informed of my progress while he was on a Naval submarine tour of duty for the past three months under the oceans somewhere in the world at the time. They were allowed to mail a type of telegram with a limited number of words to a Naval office to communicate with him every so many weeks. This Family Gram was in turn somehow secretly radioed to the sub. I guess it was a form of morale booster to the sailors on the huge nuclear submarine traversing the globe under the oceans for months at a time. I was touched that they, in their limited ability to talk to their son, were including news about me. Our next-door neighbors were definitely very nice people. Albert's father, Albert senior, gave me a good scolding; telling me not to let this thing, just an amputated foot, get me down. He told me to carry on as if it was all nothing and to just get out there and continue on with my life like nothing had changed because nothing really had. Somehow I couldn't quite understand what he meant by all that, but his efforts to help me out of my very visible sadness were greatly appreciated just because I saw that he was so genuinely concerned about me.

My buddy, Albert, was a bit wild in his overall behavior and frequently got himself in deep trouble. This is why he ended up in the Navy immediately after high school. For example, one night after he was grounded for something serious that he done, as usual, he snuck out of his bedroom window to join my brother, Ed and me. We had fun in the neighborhood that night. Albert, who was six feet tall, could buy beer for all of us, as he easily looked twenty-one years old. As the evening progressed, he drank way too much beer.

Later, in the middle of the night he had to crawl back out of his bedroom window again. This time it was to vomit in his front yard so his parents wouldn't hear him. Without his realizing it, he had crawled through some dog crap and got it all over himself as he worked his way back through the grass and up into his bedroom window and back into bed. He awoke in the morning with a lot more than a hangover. Albert had his mother screaming at him the loudest we had ever heard her. She had just found him in his bedroom, stinking to high heaven, in a room whose noxious aroma was quickly smelling up the whole house. She found him in his bed with dog crap all over it. It was all over Albert himself and even on the bedroom wall below the window. His father then gave him a kind of ultimatum about his future and it turned out that his best choice was to go ahead and join the

Navy immediately. I think for him it was probably an excellent choice. What settled me down really quickly and corrected my behavior was my foot amputation situation. Things became very serious for me very quickly. Losing a foot was like a ton of bricks falling on you all at once, weighing you down and making you feel helpless under there in the dark, not being able to move or even breathe.

After I returned from surgery I discovered who my true friends were. Only a few high school friends made sure to come and see me after they heard I was back and learned what had truly happened to me apart from the rumors. They were all my truest friends.

One of the most supportive was my friend, Ben. The doctor had told Mom that I should exercise my leg by swimming. However, when Mom and Dad talked to me about it, I told them that there was no way in hell I was going to go out to any public place anywhere to swim. To my surprise, my dad was so sensitive to my concerns that he bought and set up just for me a small aboveground pool in the backyard. I was not only impressed by this pool but also extremely thankful to my parents for it. My friend, Ben, came over and exercised with me a couple of times. I was really moved by his true friendship. He was truly one of a small group of the best of my friends.

My friend, Tim, was also a great help in my recovery. Tim was on the wrestling team with me. Veronica, his girlfriend, was voted the wrestling team sweetheart by our teammates, mostly because of her very persuasive promoter, Tim. She gave me the new "Ram" cassette tape by Paul and Linda McCartney. This was the latest release at the time. I love music and I listened to it so many times that I couldn't listen to it any more. Even Grand Funk Railroad, Deep Purple and Led Zeppelin got old fast. I was getting stir crazy, running out of things to do with my time. I guess you could say the first few weeks after the amputation I was in my own kind of Twilight Zone. The twilight was represented by my lack of direction towards a full mental recovery of all I had just been through, and the zone was my life as it was, so purposely isolated and relatively empty of anything interesting or for that matter exciting. I attempted to read a few books, painted a few things, put together a few models of cars, planes and boats. That was about it for quite a few weeks.

Another good friend, Larry, invited me to come over to his new apartment and to stay overnight. I was really ready to leave my bedroom by then out of sheer monotony. I just had to get out of the house. When he came over and picked me up in his white Pontiac Trans Am, I started to awaken finally from my twilight sleep.

The apartment he was renting was great; brand new construction, all white walls, and a nice shag rug, but sparsely furnished. Larry said some friends of his would be coming over later to hang around for a while. We were then to go on to Juarez, a neighboring city in Mexico just fifteen minutes away. We were going to a club there where other friends we knew from high school hung out on weekend nights. Suddenly I felt very queasy about being with other people socially and felt very uncomfortable about it. Larry had never said anything about these plans earlier. I had been looking forward to hanging out with Larry, but I wasn't ready for being with other people. I didn't even have an artificial leg yet. He saw that I wasn't thrilled about going out with other people, but it was too late to change the plans, so I just had to deal with it. Larry's friends showed up a few minutes later. They were a couple of guys and girls that I had never seen before, but he knew from some club he had joined. They all started talking and I tried very hard to be myself and fit right in with the group and all that was going on.

I found myself trying to hide my leg from their sight all the time. I wasn't sure whether I was doing that subconsciously or consciously, but it became rather annoying and I stopped. It was pretty funny though when the subject of conversation changed and we started talking about dreams. We talked about the strange dark fears we all seem to have in our bedrooms at certain times in our lives growing up. This one girl, Maria, said, "I used to have this fear of my hand or foot slipping over the edge of my bed during the night and it being bitten off or chopped off by some nightmarish creature that was after me." Everyone became quiet for a few seconds and I realized what had just happened. Maria's face turned bright red and she couldn't meet my eyes. Everyone looked at her in horror. She looked as if she just wanted to sink into the floor and disappear. She, and everyone else, was aghast at her insensitivity towards me. I think she was having a problem accepting me, maybe subconsciously or maybe not. I just had to say something to break the tension. "You know that's what happened to me, and look!" I said. No one laughed, but the situation ended.

It was finally time to go to Juarez, Mexico. I kept up with everyone on my crutches. That night I drank eleven shots of tequila, which was a first for me. I was still seventeen and in Mexico there is basically no drinking age. If you had money and you could reach over the countertop, you could drink all you wanted, although in El Paso it wasn't all that hard to get beer either. I expressed my frustrations by drinking to excess and numbing my brain. At the time, that was fine by me. I was still able to somehow walk back over the bridge to El Paso on my trusty crutches. I think this was a new world record for drunken-crutch-distance-bridge-walking or something like that. I was so sick the next day from all that tequila that I knew without any question that I would not be doing that again for a seriously long time. My good friend, Larry, brought me back home late the following day after sleeping it off at his place.

I finally saw that there was life outside of my bedroom though and I was very thankful to Larry for showing that to me. I just needed one thing now. I needed an artificial foot. Unfortunately, I had to wait until the next checkup appointment for it and that was still two months away. It felt like an eternity.

My birthday came in July and was pretty uneventful except for the interesting fact that now I was eighteen and still had to report to a government Selective Service office. Even though the draft had just officially ended, I still had to register; it was the law. Larry gave me a ride to the local registration office. I filled out all the appropriate paperwork and gave the papers to an angry looking red-haired lady sitting behind a little desk in the front of a huge crowded room. She thanked me as I handed her the papers. Balancing on my crutches, with only one foot under me, I asked, "When do I get my 4-F classification notice or card?" She answered in a calm, rehearsed voice, "Oh, you need a doctor's note for that." "Can't you just take a picture of me as proof of my handicapped status?" I asked. Again, she calmly said, "Please bring a doctor's note." I got the message, but I wonder if she really saw me.

I went immediately over to Dr. Goldner's office, as it was only a few blocks away. He came out to talk to me in the waiting room after seeing his patients. He literally laughed out loud when he heard about the government's request for a medical note proving my right foot had been amputated. He continued laughing as he said, "Just give me a minute;" and wrote the note. I immediately brought the note back to the same lady and thus completed my requirement as an eighteen-year-old American citizen. I completed the registration for possible future military duty and was duly registered on the 28th day of July, 1971. To my surprise, because of all of this I was feeling a bit important that day. I often felt and did say that I was such a wild soul in my youth, before I lost my foot, that if I never had lost my foot and I ever did go into the military, I probably would have gotten into a lot of trouble. I most likely would never have come back from overseas duty because I would be hiding from the military authorities way up in the mountains somewhere with two beautiful Asian women. I would be living on a farm, raising buffaloes and having the time of my life.

I needed an artificial limb now! I couldn't wait any longer for the opportunity to check out the whole experience of artificial limb-walking, of which I knew nothing about.

Chapter 9

The Artificial Limb of my Life

The next time we visited Dr. Green in Houston he examined my leg and pronounced it perfectly healed. He told me to go home and return in six months. I was surprised and disappointed that he was dismissing me so out-of-hand, without even mentioning when I would get my artificial foot. "When am I getting an artificial limb?" I demanded, the emotions churning in my stomach, making me feel a bit queasy.

"You mean no one has arranged that for you yet?" he exclaimed. My mother and I just looked at each other. Neither one of us knew what to say. After all how should we have known what to do? The doctor said that they would set up an appointment at the local prosthetic facility near the hospital complex. "I am sure they will be able to help you out and see you today," said Dr. Green, as he left us to make a phone call to them. My heart was pounding because this was so important to me and I thought, it's all going to start today, finally! With a supportive smile Dr. Green told us the appointment was set and they would take good care of me. I still knew nothing about how artificial feet were made and how they worked and as a result, I felt this tremendous anxiety about it all. I did know that an artificial limb would be a chance to move about in this world without being seen as a deformed or abnormal person. I wanted my privacy in that respect back very much. I just wanted to fit in.

After completing four years of art classes, I had learned a lot about beauty and had gained an appreciation of looking at things with a greater understanding than merely seeing what was on the surface. I was one of three students who had been considered to have natural artistic abilities and were taught separately from the rest of the students for all four high school years. We had been discovered in our freshman year by our art teacher, Mrs. Heart. Her knowledge of art and her ability to pass it on to us was truly a gift. We took full advantage of what she had to offer. As we studied great paintings and sculptures, I was taught to see the human body as a beautiful thing. As a result of my excellent art education, it was extremely difficult to accept seeing the human body mutilated in various ways. It was especially hard to accept what had been done to my own body.

In addition to all the people I had seen during my hospital experiences, I remembered seeing a veteran who liked to park his wheelchair next to the downtown movie theater in El Paso. He would just sit in his wheelchair holding a cup filled with pencils and little American flags that he would sell. He had no legs at all. I remember thinking that he looked terrible, and I wondered why he was subjecting us to the sight of him, a deformed human being with absolutely no legs. He should disappear from our sight because we all would prefer not to see him at all. I had thought this back when I had two whole legs and was also much younger. Well, now I felt like he was my brother and he had my full respect. My appearance was devoid of any kind of beauty. I wondered how an artificial limb or prosthetic device would help this sad situation, but I couldn't wait to get one so I could begin to feel whole again, and intact.

We went to the prosthetic facility immediately. Sitting in this dimly lit brown waiting room, we filled out papers as we sat and smelled faint traces of a plastic odor. Finally we were brought in for the evaluation. The prosthetist, Mr. Hall, looked at my leg with curious intent as he made notes and asked me what I would like to do after I received my prosthesis. I told him I wanted to do everything that I had done before. He told me that I would be able to do everything I did before but just not as well.

He became very concerned when he learned that we lived in El Paso. He left the room abruptly, which had me very worried. When he returned a short time later, he informed me that they would make a limb for me as quickly as possible. That news made me very happy. He added that a state run program would be paying for it in full, and that news made my mother very happy. In just three to four days I would have a finished prosthesis. I was so ecstatic I thought I would explode, and cooperated fully as Mr. Hall took measurements and made a plaster mold of my leg that he called the negative mold. The plaster had a terrible odor and felt cold and slimy. After a short time it started to heat up slowly as it stiffened.

Mr. Hall explained that he would use this mold to make my leg. First, they would pour liquid plaster into it to make the positive mold. Then the actual prosthetic device would be made from this positive mold after some very complicated adjustments to the shape were made. He told me to relax as he slipped the negative mold off my sweating leg. He looked inside the mold and studied it from different angles before declaring that it would work. We were to come back for a test socket fitting and a dynamic alignment of the rubber foot. The finished leg would be ready the next day after the adjustments were made.

My mother and I came back two days later for the fitting and alignment procedure. I was a nervous wreck as I sat in this long room with parallel bars bolted to the floor and full-length mirrors on either side. I was bursting with all this anticipation. Mr. Hall came into the room with a very serious and uneasy look on his chubby face. He had the artificial limb with him. It looked absolutely terrible. It looked like a tree trunk. It was smooth and skin colored and shaped just like a tree trunk with a foot literally glued onto it sticking out the end. My stomach was doing flips. I told myself I didn't care how it looked because my pants would cover it and no one would actually see it. He put a sock on my skin and slowly slipped the prosthesis on me. He told me to stand up mainly with my good leg and slowly ease my weight onto the prosthesis until I had equal weight on both of my legs. I robotically moved as he instructed and I then began to feel the pressure squeezing all around my leg. I was standing on two legs for the first time in months and it truly felt great to have that sense of perfect balance. He then instructed me to step out with my good foot and bring it right back to the starting point a couple of times, rocking on my prosthetic foot to get a feel for how the prosthetic foot would bend under my weight. I did this very mechanically and was just starting to get comfortable when he told me to take a step with the prosthesis. I began to walk and Mom was freaking me out as I saw her immediately start to cry. I started walking with one hand on the parallel bars first and then no hands as I saw that I had the strength in my amputated leg to control the prosthesis as my weight shifted back and forth from leg to leg.

The prosthetist gave us some advice saying that I shouldn't walk too much the first day as my knee joint would become very sore since I hadn't used it for some time. The rest of my leg that fit down in the prosthesis could also get sore from all the pressure on the skin that I wasn't accustomed to. He said the alignment looked very good and it was now time to finish it up. I asked him if he could make the leg look better and he explained that this type of leg always looked like this, although he would try to make it look the best that he could. Mr. Hall noticed that I was very concerned and said, "You see, Kevin, the device is big looking because you still have some swelling from the surgery. I had to leave room inside for you to wear a prosthetic sock to protect your skin, plus you have to account

51

for the thickness of the plastic of the device on top of all that. The combination of all these things makes the leg appear too big." He promised that as the swelling went down and the remaining muscles shrank, the future prosthetic limbs I received would begin to look a bit better because my actual remaining limb would be smaller allowing the prosthesis to be made smaller in appearance.

I asked Mr. Hall why my muscles would become smaller. He told me to call him Jim as we would be getting to know each other quite well over the next few days. He patiently explained that now that my ankle was gone, the muscles were really of no use any more so they would atrophy or slowly shrink away. I didn't like the sound of that but the knowledge that the prosthesis would look cosmetically better made it seem okay. Jim told us that we could pick up the finished prosthesis the next afternoon. As we left the clinic and waited for the bus to show up, I was smiling at the fact that I had actually walked on my prosthesis and that I did it very well, especially for the first time. Jim had been very impressed with my good sense of balance and the strength in my legs. We took a bus to shop for some baggy pants that would fit over the prosthesis. Luckily baggy pants were in fashion so the pants were abundant and we purchased a few pair.

The next day I did have a sore knee. I received my prosthesis with a supply of special socks and detailed instructions. Jim told me to be careful about what shoes I bought because the prosthesis was made for one specific heel height. If I wore shoes with a higher heel, they would tip me forward and I would not like how they would make me walk. If the heels were lower, it wouldn't be as bad but I would feel like I was walking up hill all day and I wouldn't like that either. What a lot to remember, I thought; I'd worry about all that later! I took off walking, enjoying every proud step. Jim told me to call him if I had any problems or questions.

We thanked him deeply for all his great help and we were now ready to go home to El Paso. I was going to be able to walk off the plane as a whole person, just like everyone else. I was feeling very happy! I would be walking now with a fresh new sense of appreciation for having this simple ability to walk again, something that I had always taken for granted but never would again. I was determined to walk on this prosthesis so well that people would never think that I was walking on an artificial foot and ankle!

Chapter 10

Adjusting to Life on a Prosthesis

I loved walking and had a new sense of appreciation for this newly re-acquired skill. Not only could I walk again, but I could balance myself easily standing on two feet, walk effortlessly while carrying things and best of all, no one had a clue I was an amputee. I went on long walks and did quite well. The only difficulty I encountered was that the muscles of my good leg, specifically my shin muscles on the front of my lower leg, became very sore during these long, very fast walks. Those muscles were being overworked to the point that they were straining and hurting. I learned that those muscles were the ones that pulled my foot back up as I propelled forward and pushed off my toes as I walked especially fast. They had to do the work of both legs because the artificial foot was incapable of propelling me forward at all. Unfortunately the artificial foot had no motor in it, just a simple reinforced rubber toe. My good leg was the motor, so I quickly learned that I had to strengthen it, which I did over time and things improved.

I even bravely jumped into our repaired 1968 Volkswagen Beetle one day and taught myself how to drive the "Bug" with its clutch, brake and gas pedals. The first time I told my brother, Ed, that I had driven the car he kind of freaked out a bit and asked me how I was doing it. "Let's go for a drive and I'll show you," I said, and off we went. I was making up for lost time. I showed him how I used the heel of the artificial foot on the gas and the brake pedals as necessary and used my left foot on the clutch. My shifting wasn't very smooth but I was driving again and I figured my shifting finesse would come in time, and so did Ed.

I learned to walk so well on the prosthesis that my friends and family were amazed. I was very happy to have this artificial limb and to become independently mobile again. My world was opening. I could enjoy it and live in it again because of my new limb.

My new leg fascinated me. Night after night I would lie in bed and study the artificial limb from all angles, trying to figure out how it was made. I found this new leg so intriguing and it was so challenging to try to understand how it had replaced my diseased foot. I found myself spending a considerable amount of time trying to analyze how it was made. I wondered why it looked different on the inside and had a totally different shape from the outside. Most of all I speculated about how it was actually fabricated.

Jim could have attached the rubber foot in a different place. Why had he put it specifically where he had? My mind was so stimulated by these questions that I asked them of myself over and over again. I just had this need to figure it all out. I decided the only way to really understand it all would be to get a part-time job in a place that manufactured artificial limbs, a prosthetic lab. I figured I would do this at some time in the near future and see how I might like it as a possible career.

As Jim had predicted, my remaining limb did get smaller and I developed problems with this first artificial limb. The fit of the prosthesis became very loose, losing support all around the sides of the socket, and made me take all the weight-bearing pressure right on the bottom of my remaining leg. I started developing pain as the bottom of my leg started pressing with too much pressure up against that hard plastic that made up the bottom of the prosthetic socket. The pain felt as if you had a pebble in your shoe for a whole day and you couldn't take it out so you just ignored it as long as you could until about two o'clock in the afternoon. Then it started getting so bad but you just continued to ignore it until seven o'clock at night. Then you finally took your shoe off and it was so sore that even with the shoe off it still kept on hurting just as if you were still standing on the pebble in your shoe. Hours later it would begin to settle down and go away during the night only to start the whole cycle again in the morning of the following day.

Finally I called Jim in Houston because I just couldn't take it any more. I was kind of frantic as I expressed to Jim my concern with regard to my ability to continue using the prosthesis comfortably. I was trying not to cry about it all and become uncontrollably emotional. I didn't want to lose my mobility and independence. Jim told me to go to a local limb shop in El Paso for adjustments and have them tighten the fit appropriately. He explained that they could adjust the fit to be more comfortable for me by adding padding to the inside walls in various positions.

Jim was very reassuring. He must have heard the panic in my voice as I complained to him, but he was very patient as he explained that what I was experiencing was perfectly normal and was all part of adjusting to one's first prosthesis. He reassured me that better times were coming because the shrinking process would begin to slow down soon and the proper fit of my future prosthetic limbs would last longer. I asked how long the shrinking process would take, and he told me to plan on having extreme shrinking for the next eighteen months since the process takes about eighteen months from when you receive your first prosthesis.

He told me that my leg would always shrink in volume but that I should remember that the shrinking process would slow down dramatically after that first eighteen month period of time just after the surgery. According to Jim, in the future I would easily be able to go eight to nine months without the need of any adjustments. He said I might just need simple adjustments that I could do myself, such as wearing different thicknesses of socks in various combinations to tighten the fit as my leg continued to slowly shrink as time went on. He also felt I should know that a ten pound weight gain or loss could begin to affect the comfort of the prosthesis also. I felt so much better after talking to him like my life was just restored or saved. I now knew the whole story about comfortable walking prosthetic maintenance, and most of all, that better times were coming.

My parents found a local prosthetic facility and we made an appointment. I was a little apprehensive as we approached this not too impressive looking prosthetic facility. When we were finally seen, we were told that my prosthesis needed to be replaced. I had shrunk too much for the prosthesis to be tightened enough for a proper fit. My new limb maker, Mr. Tormento, took some measurements, then looked directly at my dad as he quoted the price of a new limb.   Mr. Tormento said it would cost three hundred and eighty one dollars and he made payment arrangements with my father. When I received my new prosthesis, I was delighted to see that it was smaller in circumference than the first one.   It definitely looked much better and did not resemble a tree trunk. However, this one was aligned poorly and hurt every time I took it off.   There was some kind of hidden edge near the bottom of the socket inside that cut into me every time I removed the limb.   It was my impression that Mr. Tormento was not as skilled as Jim at making artificial limbs. He seemed to be incapable of correcting these problems even though he attempted to do so several times.

I was very angry. I had trusted that he would provide me with a proper fitting prosthesis and he hadn't.   I considered just leaving the leg on at night and never taking it off to avoid this awful pain as I tried to scrape the bone past the elusive ridge to get the leg off. Sleeping with the artificial leg would be like sleeping with your shoes on. Sure you could do it, but it wouldn't be very comfortable. One time I tried it and it was terribly uncomfortable and there was a tremendous sweat buildup. I went back several more times and Mr. Tormento couldn't figure out what was wrong. He could not fix it and he refused to make it over again. He actually said I would eventually get used to it. I didn't adjust. My hip hurt because of the improper alignment which put a constant strain on my hip joint. The prosthetic foot was positioned improperly and broke after a relatively short period of time. The foot was replaced only because it was under the manufacturer's warranty. I was glad that the company that made this particular style of lousy prosthetic foot was able to replace it; however, it just broke again in a few weeks.

The foot had some kind of a metal plate in the middle of the toe area that snapped in half and made a clicking noise when I walked. It wasn't too loud, but it clicked all day long. Most of the time it didn't bother me while walking except when I finally went on a date. It was my first date since I had the surgery. Julie was beautiful, blond, and built. As I walked Julie to her front door, all you heard was click, click, and click. It seemed that my car was parked miles from her door, not just on the street in front of her house. The night was so quiet that the click of my foot seemed to echo throughout the neighborhood. The noise ruined the romantic ending of our date. I was so embarrassed. Julie was so nice to me. She pretended not to hear the click, click, click as we strolled along, even though it was such an obvious noisy interruption to us on that quiet desert night. She invited me to come by some time and listen to music together with her and you know I did.

That atrocious prosthetic device and how it nearly ruined my evening made one thing crystal clear; it was time to get a part-time job at a prosthetic manufacturing lab. I had two reasons for wanting to do this. First, I wanted to learn how to make artificial limbs that didn't make noise on quiet romantic nights while hurting your hip as you struggled to walk and scraping the bone every time you tried to remove it. Second, and probably most important, I wanted to learn how to make a perfect one for myself, one that made walking a pleasure as it should be; not a nightmare!

Chapter 11

My Education has Started

Losing my foot helped me clarify my career goals. I already knew that I did not want to do what my family had planned for me. My uncle Jack had his dental practice in Florida and he wanted my brothers and me to move to Florida and work as dentists for him. That was the last thing on my list.

The state of Texas determined that I was handicapped so I qualified for a program that helped disabled people get jobs. Under this program, called Vocational Rehabilitation, I could go to college for free if I passed an aptitude test. If I qualified, the only thing that I would have to pay for was books. I had to take the test because my high school grades were not exceptionally good; in fact they were rather poor. I agreed to take the test. The results showed all my weak areas of educational study, or more so lack of study. No one who was involved in this process was surprised at the final results. My high school grades mirrored the test scores. I had poor English grammar, math skills, spelling skills and reading skills. After years of hearing from my parents and teachers that my school grades would affect my future, I finally realized what they were trying to tell me. How I wished that I had done better. The I.Q. score showed that I could do anything I wanted if I just put my full efforts into it and worked hard. I think that they agreed to give me a chance because my I.Q. score was high. I was so happy that I had a chance, a great chance, as I started my first semester in college at the University of Texas at El Paso.

I decided to try to get a part-time job, working in a business that made artificial limbs. I figured that I could work whenever I wasn't in class, and hoped my future employer would be amenable to such a schedule. After school started I interviewed at the two other prosthetic facilities in El Paso. I was hired immediately at one place because I agreed to sign a paper that allowed the owner to pay me only $1.00 an hour because I was a handicapped employee. Minimum wage was $1.20 an hour at the time, so I was a bargain for Burt, the owner. This was the beginning of my career in the field of prosthetics in the year 1973.

In college, I quickly became a popular student. My popularity was due to my possession of a handicapped driver sticker. This enabled me to drive anywhere on the expansive college campus and park in choice spots. Everyone wanted to ride with me after they discovered my luxury.

I had a few dates, some that went rather well and a few that didn't. One date in particular stands out in my mind. We were at the local drive-in theater when my date, Rebecca, decided to show me where her cousin had broken her leg. She grabbed my right leg in the approximate location of the break. As she made contact with the hard plastic under my pant leg, her expression grew confused as she proceeded to frantically feel up and down my leg searching for a physical explanation. She gave up trying to figure out what she was feeling and asked me about it. I explained to her that I had an artificial limb and proceeded to try and tell her about my foot amputation. She reacted like a real first-class jerk. She became quiet and really behaved like a completely different person. I took her home directly after the movie ended because I knew that was what she really wanted. I tried calling her once after that just to make sure that she was really dumping me just because of my leg. She refused to come to the phone.

Even though I tried not to let this bother me too much, it hurt an incredible amount. Later I decided that my leg would be a personality filter. It would prevent me from wasting my time talking to or being with shallow-minded, insensitive, superficial jerks. I didn't ask to have my foot amputated, and I knew that I was much more than just a guy with a missing foot. I wouldn't let other people look at me like that.

After I completed my first semester, I had worked in the limb shop enough to learn that this work demanded plenty of hands-on experience if I wanted to become great at it, and I did. At first I found it very difficult to look at other people's amputations. I was very self-conscious about looking at their limbs even though I needed to look at them as well as touch them in order to know how to fabricate the prosthesis properly. Each amputated limb looked different. I saw amputations at all levels; below the knee, above the knee, fat legs and emaciated skinny limb shapes. All were very strange to see for the first time.

I adjusted to this difficulty much faster than I thought would be possible. I was maturing and was able to look at things from a professional point of view. I was extremely pleased with myself for this major accomplishment. I felt the best course of action for my career would be to attend college at night and work full time in the limb shop. I was confident that I could do this work and do it well. I had a steadfast determination to be successful and become an excellent prosthetist. I was very fortunate to have made my career choice by the time I was nineteen. Vocational Rehabilitation agreed to continue to pay for my college courses at night and would consider paying for specialized courses at a different college if I qualified and the courses were not offered locally.

I applied to the University of California at Los Angeles, and to my great surprise my application was accepted. I found out later that I had been the youngest applicant for a prosthetic certificate course that they had ever had before. They were kind of experimenting with me. The state agreed to pay only for the Below Knee Prosthetics course tuition. I had to pay for all other expenses. My parents helped out with the rest of the arrangements. I was still living at home, so my only expense was car payments on my new metallic-green four-cylinder Pinto. I would drive to Los Angeles and stay with my Aunt Molly and Uncle Woody. I felt I was on my way to fulfilling my dream of being a prosthetist as this truly had become something I wanted to do.

Early in the morning on the first day of class, I was driving down a beautiful wide road framed with mammoth tall palm trees on either side of the street. Today I was on my way, I thought. My career was about to officially begin. As the song, *Mr. Bo jangles,* began to play on the radio, I thought that I would always remember this joyful anticipation of success every time I heard *Mr. Bo jangles* on the radio.

I found the school but panicked when I realized that I had no idea how to find the prosthetics department. I asked for directions at the bookstore. The clerk told me how to get there and after I thanked him, I flew across the sprawling campus to the prosthetic department. I couldn't be late this most important first day.

Class started with lectures on what was expected of us during this "Short Term Below Knee Prosthetics Course." They even scheduled us for an actual amputation surgery because of a procedure that was popular at the time involving what was called an immediate post-operative fitting. This involved putting a plaster fabricated socket directly onto the remaining below-the-knee amputated limb or above-the-knee amputated limb. Padding was also applied, as well as suspension straps and an adjustable pylon with a simple rubber foot attached. This was all done immediately after the surgery while the patient was still in the operating room.

The day finally came when our surgery lesson was going to happen. It was kind of cool to learn appropriate surgical room behavior and to actually see the amputation technique performed before our eyes, but this was pretty intense stuff!

In the middle of that night I woke up sweating. I had an unbelievable dream. I dreamt that I was in class having a conversation with someone for a few minutes. When I decided to turn around and finish talking, I realized the man I was talking to had no head, only a suture line across his shoulders! That only happened once and I am quite thankful for that, although I awoke one other night, but that would be for a completely different reason. There was an earthquake around 3:00 A.M. that shook the house. I realized what had awakened me when I heard about it on the news driving to school later in the morning. I survived and successfully completed the one-month course and drove myself all the way back home. Aunt Molly and Uncle Woody packed not one and not two, but three perfect salami sandwiches for my drive back to El Paso! I have always been eternally grateful for their very kind hospitality and honest concern for my well-being.

I reapplied for the next course at U.C.L.A. but I didn't get in this time. They said they had to accept people with higher educational credentials first and I was at the end of a long list.

Chapter 12

Continuing with my Education

I was disappointed that I could not continue my education immediately. The slow performance of my car was an additional frustration. I hated driving it back and forth to work, and I especially disliked driving the slow-moving vehicle on the weekends. My four-cylinder Pinto was just too slow and not very exciting to drive.

Since my boss raced formula D Rails in competition as a hobby, I asked his advice about getting a better car. "Sell your car and get the only American sports car, the Chevrolet Corvette," Melvin, my boss said. I couldn't wait to sell my car, but I wanted to make sure I would get the best price possible for it. I spent an entire Saturday cleaning my car and preparing it for sale. After cleaning and waxing my car, I used powdered cleanser and scrubbed the seats, door panels and dashboard until they all looked brand new. I was exhausted, but the car looked great. The first guy that saw it gave me my asking price, saying that the car was worth the money because it was so clean. I learned something that day; hard work does pay and pay very well.

Through the newspaper I found a 1965 Corvette Stingray (ragtop) convertible for sale. I fell in love with this car at first sight. The body style was magnificent, a real work of art. The only problem was that I needed an additional seven hundred dollars to pay for it. My dad took me to his banker and the bank loaned the money to me. Mr. Wilson, the banker, said that he was impressed with my knowledge that I would increase my car's value by fixing it up. He said he could tell I had a good work ethic and he was investing in me as much as the car.

On the third day after buying the car, I had a freak accident while stopped at a light getting ready to make a right-hand turn. The car was completely smashed on the front-end driver's side making it impossible to drive. It needed nine hundred dollars worth of repairs. I had to move back home from the apartment that I shared with my best friend, Albert, so I could save money to get the car fixed.

My boss said if I followed his instructions, he would help me completely rebuild the car into whatever I wanted. I listened to him and took advantage of the car's demolished state. I had the frame straightened and took everything apart, except for the transmission. I brought the engine parts to a race shop where they balanced the crankshaft, bored out the cylinders and put the push rods back together in a special way with a torch. I watched them do some of the work and it was quite interesting. The technician heated the push rod until the hole, which made up the top, actually expanded before my eyes. He then carefully positioned the pin that went through the piston head and held the pushrod and joined them together. He just held everything in position until the pushrod cooled and locked the three pieces together as one unit. This way there were no scratches made on any of the moving parts during the assembly process that would slow the performance of the engine.

When the engine was ready to be rebuilt, Melvin told me that he would put it together for me and install it back into the car at my house. While all this was going on I ordered a new complete front end that was designed to tilt up away from the front windshield over the front tires. With a little guidance from some car body experts I had found I installed the front-end body unit onto the car myself, setting it a little lower on the frame. It really looked awesome! The engine had become a 402 instead of a 396 and with the 1969 Camaro camshaft that my boss advised me to get, the engine sounded extremely radical.

The engine was finally ready to be put back in. First I needed to get new wheels and tires installed so my boss could test drive the car after putting the engine in. We needed to make sure the clutch and everything was working okay. Luckily my grandparents and uncle were in town for a visit and saw the car up on blocks. They wanted to know why it was in such a state. My father told them about my little mishap. They each kicked in some money so I was able to get the outrageous wide aluminum wheels and the tires I wanted. I'll always remember that, and how they came through for me.

I sanded the entire car body by hand and sprayed it with dark gray primer. It was now ready to drive. Then my friends would call me to see if they could go cruising around town with me on Friday and Saturday nights in my awesome convertible sports car. It was a nice feeling being popular for something. I had a lot of fun in that car and I was so proud of it; it was a good-looking car. I had no idea how mechanically minded I really was until after that car rebuilding and repairing experience that I truly enjoyed so much.

I had moved to Melvin's family-owned limb shop since the first one I had been working in had become boring. They had me doing the same things every day and I felt I wasn't growing or gaining the skills that I would need in the future. My new job offered me an opportunity to expand my knowledge and go further ahead in my chosen career and I was guaranteed an opportunity to learn. I applied to Northwestern University in Chicago since it felt like U.C.L.A. had abandoned me. I had heard nothing from them in quite a while.

I was thrilled when I received a call from the Northwestern University registration office one morning as I was working at the limb shop. I was accepted into the program, providing I could raise the three thousand dollars for tuition. The admissions people at Northwestern were impressed that I had successfully completed the Below Knee course at U.C.L.A. and that's why they were offering me this opportunity to attend their new long-term certificate program. I asked the registration office to hold my spot because I was going to attend no matter what, and assured them that I would be sending the tuition money before the deadline. When I completed the ten-month long program, I would be in a position to qualify for the National Board for Certification in Orthotics and Prosthetics examination. When I passed, I would be a Certified Prosthetist or C.P.

I told my mom and dad, who didn't have the money, that somehow I was going to Chicago because there was no way that I was passing up this opportunity. Next I set up an appointment with the state vocational rehabilitation office counselor to see if he could help out and allow me to finish my prosthetic education. My counselor, Tom, said he could not authorize that kind of money for a one-time tuition expense. I was upset, of course, but he immediately said, with a thoughtful smile on his face, "The district manager is coming into town next week and he could authorize this for you!" Tom said he would call him to see if he would allow me to have an appointment with him to discuss my situation. I felt I had a chance now but it didn't matter, because even if that didn't work out, I would find a way no matter what. I was that determined and I had complete confidence that I would be attending.

Tom told me that the district manager had invited me to have lunch with him. I accepted quite nervously. During that lunch appointment Mr. Biggens, the district manager, asked me several quite personal questions and I answered them all very respectfully. I understood that he was checking me out to see if I was worthy of this expensive level of financial aid. I also informed him that my ultimate dream was to own and manage my own prosthetic company.

Finally he asked me why I wanted this opportunity so much. I told him that I felt I had a lot to offer amputees since, as an amputee, I could easily demonstrate to my new amputee patients how well they could be walking.

I explained that I had a unique understanding of how I would help them get back to a normal lifestyle by providing them with properly designed limbs. Seeing my patients happily walking on a limb that I had made for them would always cause me to feel very satisfied inside, I added, and this would be very rewarding for me all through my life as a certified prosthetist. Mr. Biggens grew quiet and I grew nervous. I prayed he would say yes. After a thoughtful delay he said, "I am sending you to the Northwestern program in Chicago because I like very much your honest and sincere determination to be successful in the career you have chosen for yourself. I know you will be successful in the prosthetic program and I am doing this because I want Vocational Rehab to be a part of your success."

He reminded me that they would be paying only for the tuition and the rest of the expenses would be my responsibility. After I told my father all this, he took out a loan on some insurance policies he had to cover my food, books, transportation and lodging expenses. Before I could get my thank you's out of my mouth Dad told me that I would have to repay the loan, which was about seven hundred and fifty dollars, the total estimated extra expenses. I accepted my father's terms happily and for the first time realized I was actually going. I was being given a chance to bring my dream to reality. Soon I would be able to sit for the certification exam by the American Board for Certification in Prosthetics and become a prosthetist. Even my ultimate goal of having my own prosthetic manufacturing facility was finally within my reach.

Chapter 13

Going to Chicago, the Big City

I needed to leave my beautiful 1965 Corvette behind as I set off for Chicago. Reluctantly, I put it back up on blocks. My brother, Eric, was charged with starting it up once a week and letting that outrageous engine run for about ten minutes or so. Although, he agreed to do so a little too eagerly for my comfort, I knew that since he was five years younger than me I could threaten him just enough to ensure that he would do as I asked without trying to take the car for a joyride, so to speak, in my absence. My brother also promised to look after my little black and white dog, Harlequin. She was the cute offspring of the two dogs, Peanuts and Shaina, my parents had for us. Harlequin was a good dog, and smart. I knew I would miss that small, shorthaired, black and white dog while I was gone and she would miss me. Finally, my trunk was packed with all that I would need for a ten month sojourn to the "Windy City" and I was off to the airport.

The snow was falling lightly when I arrived in Chicago. It was a treat for me to see all the white stuff because I had not seen snow since we had moved from Cleveland when I was ten. I didn't count the rare snow flurries that infrequently swirled around the El Paso streets. I caught a bus and asked to be dropped at the downtown Y.M.C.A. The driver watched impassively as I struggled to get my overloaded trunk onto the bus. He motioned for me to leave the trunk on the side and not try to maneuver it down the aisle. I took a seat and watched the city go by as the bus meandered all over town. I was the last one left on the bus, when much to my surprise; the driver dropped me off right in front of the Y.M.C.A. even though it wasn't an official bus stop. I guess he must have felt sorry for me, lugging my trunk on a bus and staying at the "Y".

I checked into the "Y" and after paying for my first week in advance. I was shown to a tiny room that was barely large enough to hold a bed, sink, clothes closet and small chest of drawers. The bathroom was down the hall. Everything felt extremely weird!

I was very uneasy about this whole Y.M.C.A. experience. I made the mistake of arriving two weeks early to study anatomy in order to prepare myself for the start of the prosthetic program. I was extremely excited about the whole experience and couldn't wait to get started.

I could not believe how quickly I became so devastatingly lonely. When my parents called me every couple of days, I couldn't wait to speak to them. As a typical teenager, I couldn't believe that I wanted to talk to my parents. Loneliness was a new feeling for me. I had never been all alone before. I was in this huge great city with millions of people, and I knew absolutely no one at all. I had never been so lonely. Having no one to talk to all day wore me down. I felt so isolated and alone in this great sea of people. Going out, walking around and then coming back to my little room and seeing that I had no one to share my experiences of the day with, was very depressing. I couldn't get used to it. Having the company of another human being sounds so simple and trivial, but it is a pleasure that I would not do without after experiencing this. I felt very depressed and counted the days until school would start.

I learned something about loneliness though. I quickly developed a new respect for the sadness that I knew so many people face every day because they have no one with whom to share their day-to-day lives. The "Y" was a strange place to live. I couldn't become accustomed to it. Just getting in the elevator was scary because you never knew who would be joining you for the brief ride up or down. Extremely bizarre people lived there and friendliness was not their thing. During my brief stay there prior to school starting, two girls jumped out of a window together and committed suicide. As I read about it the next day, I realized that I never would have known that it actually happened if I hadn't seen it in the newspaper. It had happened during the night; I never heard a thing and I was glad about that.

As I was flipping through the newspaper that day, I came to an interesting article describing different true wills and testaments that people left their loved ones. I remember one really funny one and it went like this: "When I die, my wife cannot inherit any part of my estate until she gets remarried. In this way I will know that there will be at least one person on this earth that really wishes I was still alive!" Amazing I thought, how creative, but kind of an angry thing to write in one's last will and testament. His wife must have been a real trip to live with! I knew that I wanted to live a happy life and keep moving in a direction that would bring me happiness throughout my life. My goal was to have a happy and peaceful life, and definitely have someone to share the good times and the bad.

I ate in some truly terrible restaurants that were astonishingly busy. I figured that their downtown locations allowed them to cater to so many people that even if each customer came in once and never came back again, it really didn't matter to them. The constant flow of new people kept them busy enough to stay open. Instead of seeing me as a customer I felt that the wait staff saw me as an inconvenience. I didn't understand their attitude. The cafeteria in the "Y" wasn't so bad until the cashier started looking at me in a very weird way and wanted to give me unasked-for discounts on my food.

I couldn't wait for school to start. I really hoped that they might let me make a new prosthesis, one that I would be able to make for myself. I couldn't wait until we studied the Syme type amputation prosthesis. Melvin, my last boss, had made my most recent replacement prosthesis because Vocational Rehabilitation agreed to pay for it. However, my limb had shrunk in size again and badly needed to be replaced so I could keep working, walking and learning comfortably. The defectively fitting device caused me to walk poorly. It wasn't the right length. The foot was not aligned properly. The socket fit had become too big, and was once again causing painful pressure areas inside. Making matters worse, my right hip hurt all the time. This was actually my third prosthesis and I hadn't had much luck getting a good one yet. The less I walked, the better I felt.

When I first received this prosthesis, it was decent enough. It had enabled me to prove to myself and to my friends how much I could do after the amputation. For example, one weekend my friend, Tim, had invited me and two other friends to drive with him up to Ruidoso, New Mexico, to go fishing and camping. We drove up there from El Paso and paid a small fee to camp along a tiny creek on Indian land. We were actually on the Apache reservation, which was in the southern part of New Mexico. We unloaded our camping gear. Tim, our self-proclaimed leader and chief, instructed us to move along the creek until we found a good campsite deep in the woods on this fantastic mountainside. The trees were so beautiful and dense. The wind whistled as it moved through them. The smell of crisp fresh mountain air was awesome.

We walked and walked and walked until I started getting a reminder that I was walking on an artificial limb. It was too soon to stop. I couldn't bear the thought of having us all stop because I was crying about my sore leg. These were good guys and they would have taken a break for me without asking any questions, but I decided to ignore the pain and walk, and walk even faster. I soon took the lead still holding my fishing rod in one hand and my sleeping bag, laden with supplies, in the other. I walked as if I was Superman, totally immune to pain. I wanted to feel like a tough young man instead of a wimp. I halted at a turn in the creek because it had a nice open flat area with some big rocks to the side that would provide shelter if it rained. I waited at this potential campsite for the others to catch up and see if they agreed that I had found an acceptable campsite. Tim showed up first and said, "Man, I thought you would never stop, this is far enough, let's camp right here man!"

We set up camp and we all proceeded to have a great time fishing, sneaking up on the local trout as they hid under the rocks at the sides of the creek. It was so cool sneaking up to cast a tiny silver spinner out into a small crystal clear pool in the creek. It looked completely void of all life, and then bam! three to five trout came out of nowhere to bite. Catching and cooking them for our dinner that night was really a lot of great fun and excellent eating. We finished setting up our campsite. Being up in the mountains, exhausted but enjoying the whole experience, relaxing into the night, joking around and telling stories is a memory that I'll always treasure. That day I felt fully accepted by my friends as an equal, despite my disability. I liked that very much. I knew that I could do even better with a better artificial leg! My buddies never knew about the huge blister I developed just under my knee cap though. By the morning I felt a lot better and with a fresh prosthetic sock on, I was up for another glorious day.

I even went water-skiing with this leg. Tim and Veronica had invited me to join them on Veronica's dad's boat. Tim had helped me figure out how to water-ski with my prosthesis on. I really liked seeing his genuine excitement as he saw me slalom on the one ski with my artificial limb jammed in the back foot holder. My good foot was first set in the front. I was doing quite well until the rubber part of the foot came unglued and I lost control tumbling into the cold water for the last time that day. I absolutely love water-skiing. It was something that I never thought I'd be able to do after the amputation. I have Tim to thank for showing me how to do that, and also Veronica and her dad.

School finally started and it was with a great sense of relief that I was able to leave the "Y". I moved in with two students who were also in the prosthetic program. They had rented a large three-bedroom apartment in a little city just north of Chicago. The guy they had planned to room with never made it into the school program and they needed a roommate. After begging these two guys for several days, they finally consented to letting me be their new roommate. I was so glad to leave the "Y". Living conditions just got a whole lot better.

Chapter 14

The Prosthetic Program Begins

I wasn't sure what to expect as I took the elevator up to the seventeenth floor of the Rehab Institute of Chicago. The view from the top of the building was awesome. As I entered the classroom and looked out the massive windows, I could almost see clear across Lake Michigan. I felt like I was floating amongst the clouds. The instructor quickly brought me down to earth as he proclaimed, "You better pick up all the books on this list as soon as possible because starting tomorrow you are expected to know everything in all of them. I can assure you that you will be tested to prove that you comprehend all you should know." The instructor passed out the course syllabus and reading list and I knew that any illusions of partying while I was in Chicago were out of the question.

Every day there were endless lectures and lab work. My favorite part of the day turned out to be lunch. The most challenging part of the day was something called Critique. During Critique you had to present your patient in front of the entire class and staff, demonstrating how the device you had just made for your professional patient worked and how perfectly it performed its intended functions. I always wanted to be the best in the class and felt tremendous pressure to succeed.

My fellow students called me the Texan for the obvious reason that I came from Texas. A simple math problem helped me impress my classmates. One day during the first week of prosthetic school, I was relaxing with my head on my arms on the chair desktop surface. I was just waiting for the professor to show up for an early morning lecture. One of my roommates was trying to calculate the costs involved in our rental agreement when he shouted out from across the room, "Kevin, what's two hundred and fifty one divided by three?" Without any hesitation, I replied, "eighty three point six, six, six, six, six." That simple repeating decimal was an easy calculation for me, but the other students who had heard our conversation were very impressed with my lightning quick ability to calculate all those sixes. As the program progressed, my serious devotion to the profession was what earned me true respect from my fellow students. Although I quickly settled into the routine of the program, I was still nervous about the daily quizzes and questions provided by our instructors. However, I enjoyed the prosthetic program very much all the same.

Todd, one of my fellow students, would always check out the new professional patients waiting for us before we started experimenting on them. He would then let us know which one would prove to be the greatest challenge. The patients changed as we learned about the different types of prosthetic devices required for different types of amputations. The school paid the patients to allow us to work on them. Regardless of what they earned, I thought they were very courageous to let us basically experiment on them.

It was an honor to have the most challenging cases assigned to you since that meant that the professors thought your past performances were worthy of a greater challenge. Often, I was given the most difficult cases. My professors held me in high regard and seemed interested in ensuring that I received the best possible education.

The lab part of school was easy for me because I had had three years of on-the-job training before starting the program. Most of the students in the program, like my two roommates, Terry and Daniel, were academically well-versed but had little or no lab experience. I would quickly finish my lab work and get home by mid-afternoon and have plenty of time to study the theories, biomechanics and anatomy that were necessary to learn. My roommates would roll into the apartment as late as eight o'clock, exhausted after finishing their lab work or fabrication. They looked like hell, their clothes covered in ground plastic dust, the smell clinging to them.

I just loved lunch. As the morning progressed, I would develop such a hunger that I would feel more and more uncomfortable as lunchtime approached. After finally eating my simple lunch I would feel so good that I would kind of Zen out on the wonderful satisfied feeling I was experiencing. I would just lean back in the booth and close my eyes. I would then deeply relax using this feeling in my stomach as a platform for a peaceful escape from the soul-crushing stress.

One day as we strolled back into the lecture room after lunch, we saw Todd, our fellow student, walking up to us. He was very upset and nervous as he told us that we were about to get our above-the-elbow amputation patients. I couldn't understand why Todd was so upset, since we had known about this prior to lunch. "One of the patients has no face!" he stammered, explaining that the patient was a burn victim. The three of us looked at each other, shocked and nervous about what to expect. "The guy looks really bad." he said.

"Go and find out his name so we can see who is getting him," I said. On the center back wall of the lab was a big chalkboard where the names of the students and their corresponding patients were posted. No one wanted to be the one to have to work with the burn victim. Todd was soon running back to where we were all frozen in place. The burn victim had a name now, Samson. Slowly we went into the lab, wondering who would have to deal with Samson. I raised my eyes to look at the board, and my heart sank. My name was the one written next to his. Panic flowed over me with a rush of adrenalin almost like an emersion into a liquid pool of electricity.

Like a condemned man, I walked slowly to my workbench and started gathering my measuring devices and measurement forms as I tried to get organized. The other students weren't very helpful. Unwanted, unnecessary comments filled the room as the others worked off their relief at not having to face Samson. My schoolmates were definitely not being very sensitive about this situation. I pulled myself together and robotically entered the patient area. I went through the motions I needed to accomplish the goal for that day. I had to take a cast and measurements for an above-elbow prosthetic device. I think this was a defining moment in my professional development. I had to face my fears about dealing with severely deformed individuals.

Samson's face was a mass of scar tissue. His nose was just two little holes in the middle of what had once been a face. His eyes were devoid of expression. No trace of emotion could be detected through the mask of scar tissue. He had no lips to frame his distorted mouth opening. I was truly scared of this guy and a total nervous wreck. His chest, as well as his above-elbow amputation on the left side, were all scarred. Even his armpit was marked by the fire that had maimed him. I began to realize that my professors had actually given me a gift, since this was an extremely difficult case to fit successfully with a comfortable prosthesis of any type. I would also have to learn how to look at the patient and talk to him in a respectful professional manner.

As I worked preparing Samson's artificial limb, his deep-seated anger became apparent and I definitely experienced it firsthand. One morning, while testing the function of the prosthetic arm, I politely asked him to slowly extend the prosthetic elbow straight out with the stainless steel hook on the end of the forearm section. He just looked at me and then abruptly extended it almost hitting me in the nose with the hook. It missed me by only the distance of a hair. I could tell that he meant to do it. It wasn't an accident!

Eventually we all got used to his appearance and enjoyed riding with him in the elevator to the cafeteria for lunch. We would watch the people's faces as the elevator door opened on each floor. People who saw him for the first time reacted differently. We didn't know what expression we would see on their faces as the elevator door stopped on the long journey from the seventeenth to the second floor. We found their reactions most interesting and educational. Some people would just turn away quickly in shock; some looked actually horrified and kept staring at him; some just looked at him with very sad eyes almost with tears forming.

I made him an acceptable arm. My classmates discussed my work in Critique class and agreed the device was acceptable. I did very well throughout the upper extremity classes as well as the lower extremity ones. I was extremely proud that I excelled in the special prosthetics courses. These were very complex cases, such as developing prosthetics to replace the entire limb due to the removal of the entire thigh bone; in rare cases even half of the pelvic bone. More importantly I felt very good about the fact that I was growing as a young man, conquering my fears and starting well on the difficult road to becoming a true professional. I felt good knowing that I would soon be called a "Certified Prosthetist" having earned the right to put C.P. after my name.

One afternoon while we were working on making a complicated below-the-knee prosthesis, I learned a valuable lesson beyond the mechanics of fashioning artificial limbs. The device we were working on this day consisted of a leather thigh corset attached to external knee joints. We had to position the lower half of the joints carefully on the prosthetic socket in just the right place. It was very time consuming and stressful to create this type of complicated device properly. I saw one student, Samuel, have his corset with the joints already attached get ripped out of his hands into the high-powered sanding machine. It went around and around several times before throwing one joint and then the other up into the air. When he finally turned off the machine, his damaged corset just fell to the floor as a jumbled scratched-up mess. I felt badly for him but had to press on as I had my own problems doing my own work well. I was consoling my fellow student while still working on my corset. Professor Gibson, a thin, older European man, walked over and started lecturing us. He went on about how as prosthetists we would be the difference between pain and comfort for our patients as we provided them with finished prosthetic devices.

I was outraged to think that this man who still had all his limbs could truly understand what an amputee feels. "How would you know anything about what pain an amputee feels, you're not an amputee," I proclaimed with a loud voice. He grabbed my arm and pulled me into an adjacent empty room. He pushed me up against a wall by my shoulders as he kept saying over and over again, "I know what it feels like, I know, I know." His face was an inch away from mine. His angry eyes blazed directly into me, convincing me of his true deep sincerity. I realized that I was just a hotshot young student with a big mouth totally out of line. Professor Gibson did teach me that someone could be a sincere and excellent prosthetist without being an amputee. I had a newfound respect for the true professionals out there working in the field of prosthetics with all their limbs intact. I completed the device I was making and passed the critique.

I finally had the opportunity to make a new prosthesis for myself. My friends helped me with the alignment of the foot and I did all the fabrication. It was a very good prosthesis. I walked very well on it to prove that point. It was the most comfortable device I had ever used. I was very proud that I had fashioned it. I also finally finished my term paper which was titled, "The Physiological Adjustment to a Prosthesis."

I had chosen that one because I wanted to learn more about myself and discover what I could about my own physiological adjustment. I'll tell you I had my own problems because I would feel pretty pissed off from time to time about the fact that I was an amputee. I was especially annoyed when I saw how some things that had come easily to me before no longer did; simple things, like dancing for example, that needed some finesse. I was totally lacking the finesse necessary to perform a task like dancing well. I could still dance, but not as well as my friends could. It hurt me deeply to see them bouncing and twirling effortlessly with the girls, who obviously enjoyed dancing with them so much. The prosthesis was definitely not a real foot and ankle. It could never offer the control necessary to perform tasks that really needed precision and elegance. The fact that I was a perfectionist wasn't helping either. That reality was disturbing to me and was a definite part of my struggle with regard to fully accepting the amputation of *my* foot and the use of *my* prosthetic device.

The program came to an end and I successfully completed all that was asked of me as a prosthetic student. I even passed the test to become a provider of services for the Veterans Administration and I felt exceedingly happy about that. I was one of the highest achieving students and I was very proud of that achievement also. I was really feeling great about myself and I experienced an excellent feeling of completion. Unfortunately, I had miscalculated my finances and had to borrow ten dollars from Daniel. I had to vow seriously to pay him back immediately after I arrived home. He begrudgingly loaned the money to me and I thanked him most sincerely. I now had just enough money

for transportation back to the airport so I could then eagerly
fly back to my home in El Paso.

Chapter 15

Preparing to Move On

Soon after I returned home, I reported to the Vocational Rehabilitation Office in downtown El Paso. Everyone in the office stood up and applauded as I entered. They were so proud that I had successfully completed the program and that I was now ready to be a productive member of society. I hadn't realized that many of the people that the Rehabilitation Office tries to help never complete the courses they start. That makes the organization look very bad, almost as if the organization is wasting the federal funds meant to help educate local disabled people. This occurs simply because the people they are trying to help don't finish what they start. I personally feel that this organization is very beneficial, because the government actually gets back all the money they spend on you. After you start working, you begin paying income taxes and the government gets their money back. The government actually invests in people and you don't have to think of it as charity.

My counselor, Tom, insisted that I sit down and write a letter to the Texas State Governor's office. He wanted me to tell the governor how important the Vocational Rehabilitation program was to me and should always be to the state and federal government. I wrote everything he wanted me to write and happily finished the letter. Tom was extremely delighted with me, especially because he could consider my case successfully closed. It was very nice to see how important that was to him.

My car was running great and I was ready to collect all my things and set out for new horizons. El Paso offered me very little. My previous boss said I could have my old job back, but I would be doing the exact same things as I had been doing prior to prosthetic school. I understood that was all he could offer me, so I wasn't interested. If I stayed under those conditions, I would not be able to continue growing as a professional. I needed patient contact experience. I graciously declined Melvin's offer to stay and left on good terms with him, thanking him sincerely for all he had taught me. I'll never forget what he used to say when he was trying to teach me something. "I am only going to tell you this once so you better listen," he would say. Another favorite expression of his was, "I am only going to show you this once so you better pay close attention!"

I accepted an offer to work in Evansville, Indiana, with the opportunity to have the full patient contact experience I needed. I still needed a few more college classes to complete my prerequisites so I could sit for the professional national exam through the American Board for Certification. I decided to register at the local state college, Indiana State University of Evansville, after I had settled in. Harlequin and I drove off for Evansville with all my possessions and that was to be my last time in El Paso for a long while.

The car drove beautifully and I enjoyed the long drive with the top down most of the way. I moved along north through the beautiful Texas landscape that seemed to continually spread out before my tired eyes. The wind blowing through my hair exhilarated me and was my constant companion as I flew along the highway. I prayed for the next part of my life to develop as I looked ahead. I felt very good about my accomplishments to date and couldn't wait to get started with my new job as an interning prosthetist.

Suddenly I realized that it was pitch black and I was in the middle of nowhere, totally exposed with the convertible's top down. The night noises sounded quite strange, and this made me decide to pull over and put the top up. Who knew what kind of night-flying animals lurked out here in the wide-open Texas wilderness, I thought. I slowed, pulled off the highway, stopped, jumped out and hurriedly pulled the top up, locked it down, jumped back in, closed the door, and rolled up the windows faster than an electric window could travel up. I then sped off. I continued on to my overnight stay destination definitely feeling better, even though the convertible top didn't really offer much protection. Finally arriving in Evansville I stayed in a motel that offered daily and weekly room rentals.

I was going to start my new job the next morning. That night, as I lay in bed, I thought about how far I had come with the development of my prosthetic education up to this point. I was feeling pretty well balanced, pursuing a career and succeeding in it. I was happy about the direction I was taking. Moving to this strange place though was giving me a tremendous amount of anxiety! Maybe I should have felt a bit off balance and unsure about what I wanted to do with my life. I did feel confident with my decisions. I felt that I knew what would be expected of me by the patients, and of course, my new boss, and this helped. I honestly felt fine. I knew I could be a great prosthetist and that I enjoyed the profession very much. I felt solid, with two good supportive legs firmly on the ground under me.

I was ready to learn all I could about my profession, a profession of my choosing, a great profession that offered a renewed life of functional possibilities for all amputees. I was ready for the next step in my evolution as an up and coming young prosthetist. I planned on being very respectful to my new boss, hoping he would like me immensely as he learned more about me while we worked together. I hoped that he might be motivated to help me to learn all I needed to know. I wanted so much to accomplish my goal of becoming a Certified Prosthetist and making superior limbs for people in need. My ultimate goal, that I was just starting to dream of quite seriously, was to one day, dare I think, actually have my very own prosthetic facility.

I was extremely excited and completely optimistic about my Evansville work experience to come that it was almost impossible to sleep. With my career path firmly established, I reevaluated my complete life's dreams. I thought about marriage and family. I was sure that one day I would get married to a beautiful and wonderful woman, a sexy angel with long hair. We would meet one day soon and I would love her eternally. I decided that my dream girl would have to work in the health care field so we could share our workday experiences. In this way we could have a full understanding of each other's workday as we enjoyed our lives together. I wanted a woman who cared about our health completely and lovingly and consistently cooked healthy meals for our family. I felt that if I ate properly, meaning never eating anything in excess, I could possibly lessen my risk of getting that damn cancer ever again. I wanted to have at least four children so there wouldn't be one child in the middle like I was, because it was downright brutal at times growing up with my two brothers. Also, if something would ever happen to their mother or me they would always have each other to share their lives with.

I desperately wanted to do well financially so it would be possible for us to travel around the world with the children. I wanted to expose them to the great educational opportunities available. Of course, I wanted to always have a great sports car to drive every day of the week and an ultra-great quadraphonic stereo system.

I passionately wanted to always make great artificial limbs and I was discovering that making proper artificial limbs is truly a very complicated process. I wanted to master this process over time so that one day I would be able to provide exceptional prosthetics and do it in my own prosthetic facility. I had a lot to learn and I knew that bigger paychecks would come in time as my skills continued to develop. I just needed to be patient and learn all I could. Boy, I thought, I sure do want a lot, don't I? Sleep finally enveloped me and I began the recharging process that deep restful sleep brings.

My new boss, Cooter Smith, turned out to be an amputee himself and a tremendously laid back nice guy. A big corporation that owned many medical facilities across the country owned this facility also. Smith was the manager for this location. He asked where I was staying and when he heard that I had no place rented long term as yet, he recommended that I speak to the owner of the building that the facility was in. It turned out that there was a furnished apartment upstairs which was available for rent. I immediately made an appointment with the landlord to see about getting that apartment. It turned out to be a great deal. Since I agreed to paint the place and put up some wallpaper, I would only be charged twenty five dollars a month in rent. We had a deal with a handshake and I was thrilled that there would be no driving back and forth to work, just running up and down the stairs. The low rent would also make it possible for me to pay my dad back the money I owed him much faster. This all made me very happy.

Chapter 16

My Prosthetic Residency Has begun

I learned a lot working with Cooter, especially upper extremity prosthetics because I was now living in the Corn Belt with a lot of hard-working farmers around. Unfortunately, farm related injuries were abundant. These were very challenging cases mostly involving arms due to the nature of the dangerous equipment the farmers had to use daily. I remember one nice man who had been electrocuted while working on his farm. He had lost both his feet, one arm just below the elbow, and also one eye as a direct result of the electrocution. Sam Mc Dermate was the toughest man that I had ever met at this point in my life. He came in one day needing repairs to his right prosthetic arm. Sam had been installing fence posts and had broken a control cable on his very short below-elbow amputation type arm. This man managed his own farm and took care of his family. He was a big muscular man and he had two small children. We simply repaired the broken cable and had a very nice visit with a satisfied patient.

One of my first lower extremity patients turned out to be a very nervous man who had a below-the-knee amputation on the right side. My boss thought he would be another good patient for me to take care of. By then I had taken care of a couple of patients and Cooter had gained some confidence in me. He started giving me the opportunity to learn how to fit amputees with prosthetics through direct patient contact. It was exactly the learning experience which I had hoped for. When this patient came back to test the fit and then the foot alignment, I found quite quickly that I had messed up. I slipped his leg onto him and when he stood up on it, he literally started jumping up and down frantically on this new leg! He was trying to force his short remaining limb into the custom-made prosthetic socket I had created for him. The whole time he was jumping he was saying over and over again, "This is the worst leg I have ever had." I finally got him to sit back down and asked him to take the leg off. I wanted to go back into the lab and figure out what needed to be done to correct the fit. As I was leaving the room, he said, "You should toss it in the garbage because it's crap."

After much examination I discovered that I had put my other patient's left below-knee socket onto *his* right foot. I was so inexperienced that I had put a left patient's socket onto his right foot and because of my naïveté I couldn't tell just by looking at the sockets. An experienced prosthetist could easily have seen the difference between a right below-knee socket and a left one. I quickly switched the sockets that did deceivingly look very similar to my as yet untrained eye. When I had Mr. Fuming try the fit again he said, "That's more like it, yes!"

I learned a lot that day but the stress of the experience had me completely exhausted. I was ready to go upstairs and just crash out. I did end up going to bed early that night. I realized while I lay in bed thinking about the day and evaluating how I had performed, that in order to make this job less stressful, I needed to learn how to create these very complicated devices properly. It would be good for the patients, of course, and good for me emotionally. I knew if I did my best and constantly worked to improve myself, I'd be able to sleep at night with a clear conscience, knowing I had done my best and that my patients were happy. I cared very much about my prosthetic work and only wanted it to improve continuously. If I could do this, I knew that I would always earn and deserve my patients' trust in me and that was the most important thing. I learned that if my patients didn't fully trust me, my experience with them would be most difficult and probably lead to failure on my part.

I found out about one of the worst mistakes I had made when one of my above-the-knee patients came back in one day with this terrible story. He complained to Cooter loudly enough on purpose for me to hear him quite clearly as I worked in an adjacent room. He went on to tell my boss how he had been walking in the biggest grocery store in town doing his shopping. He was pushing a cart down the wide aisle in the pet food section when he had felt his foot loosen abruptly and then click off while he walked. The foot then unexpectedly rolled out into the middle of the aisle as he fell against the cart. A lady in front of him, who was carrying several cans of dog food in her hands, saw the foot roll out in the middle of the aisle. She immediately dropped all the dog food cans and nearly convulsed as she observed this unbelievable spectacle. I repeatedly apologized to our patient, Mr. Truckner, and was eventually absolved of my errors since I was still interning.

It was expected that I would make mistakes, but it was important that I learned from them. The new type of connection design for modular component parts that was in Mr. Truckner's above-knee prosthesis had four sides. There is an Allen screw on each side that holds his leg together at various points. This part of the connection with the Allen screws is called the female side, as the male side has a four-sided block of metal that fits exactly inside the female side. As you tighten each Allen screw in each side independently, it locks down very well because the metal block has a slight pyramid taper to it that forces both pieces together nicely. In some above-knee type prosthetic devices there are four of these male and female connectors. One attachment is below the socket, one above the prosthetic knee, one below the knee and one above the foot and ankle. There is an aluminum pylon or pipe sandwiched in between all of them, thus completing the thigh and shin sections. With all of these connectors you could then adjust the alignment of the

91

leg in twenty different directions not counting the actual knee motion control adjustments. Below-the-knee limbs in most cases have only twelve separate adjustments because there are only two alienable connectors being used.

I had just learned, to Mr. Truckner's misfortune, that if you tighten the Allen screws without putting forth careful attention, you could cause the attachment to wedge together improperly simulating a properly tightened attachment. All it took was time until the parts would jump back into their proper fitting positions with respect to each other. The attachment would then loosen and continue loosening with the aid of the vibration caused naturally with each step thereafter. I had also been learning quite slowly about alignment in general. The final position of the prosthetic knee joint alignment as well as the foot in the finished prosthesis always had to be located in the most correct alienable position possible. No matter how advanced the prosthetic parts may be, if they are not aligned correctly under the patient's body, the patient will never be able to benefit from them as he/she should. This would continue to happen no matter how hard he/she might try to walk properly.

I realized that I had to learn proper alignment, since next to the actual socket fit it was the most important part of making efficient, properly working prosthetic devices. It ended up taking me about three years to master this part of the limb making process.

I attended Indiana State University at Evansville nightly until I finally successfully completed my educational requirements. The women on that huge campus were so beautiful that I couldn't believe my eyes. Unfortunately, I never had good relationships develop, much to my dismay.

I received my invitation to sit for the prosthetic board's exam in 1979 when I had finally met the full educational requirements. Reality struck and I instantly became a nervous wreck. I was freaking out about this examination which was all that stood between the completion of my professional career education and me. I read that the exam, which was scheduled to take place in Chicago, spanned over two days. It included a practical exam one day and an oral exam the second day. I had already taken and passed the written exam while I had been in prosthetic school and that had entitled me to take the other two exams. Once those exams were successfully completed I would become a Certified Prosthetist or, "C.P.", and that had always been my goal.

I will never forget opening the letter the exam board sent after I sat for the boards. I had waited months to learn whether or not I had passed. That day I saw Cooter walking over to me with a great big smile, carrying a letter. He looked extremely happy as he handed me the letter and I was confused as to why he was smiling so much. The letter was addressed to me, of course, but there were those two little letters, "C.P.", after my name. I was thrilled to see "Kevin S. Garrison, C.P." in print for the first time. Most important was that meant I had made it. It was great having Cooter hand me the letter after he sorted through the mail that day. He presented it to me with his own profound personal joy for *my* accomplishment. He knew how important it was to me.

I really liked Cooter, my boss, very much because he offered me such an excellent opportunity, allowing me to learn under his supervision. Apparently Cooter thought I was management material and without me knowing it, he had told this to his boss, Mr. Curray. The next thing I knew, upper management wanted me to transfer to their Chicago office to be groomed to assume the management of that office some day in the future. I accepted the offer with guarded optimism though, and began planning my departure from Evansville, coordinating with Cooter and my landlord. Leaving Evansville was very difficult for me and I think

Cooter also, but I needed to move on and Cooter knew this most of all. I was returning to Chicago, only this time I knew people who lived there. I was somewhat familiar with the big city now and I was a Certified Prosthetist ready to continue the development of my prosthetic career with enthusiasm. I smiled as I realized what a long way I had come since my first visit.

ROBERT H. PERRY—Painter, Hudson Co., N.J.
Above knee.

I am still wearing the leg you furnished eighteen years ago. I have worn it comfortably with less than six dollars cost for repairs. My occupation (house painter) gives it a good test. I can and do work on scaffolds, ladders—in fact, anywhere. I have but a three-inch stump. I am well satisfied.   Oct. 16, 1909

Illustration (1)

FRANK TRIACCA—Schoolboy, Fairfield Co., Conn.
Below knees.

I am going to school every day and walk both ways.
My artificial legs give the best of satisfaction in every way
and have proved a great benefit to me. I walk, run, and play
as well as most boys. When I tell persons that both of my
legs are artificial, they will not believe me until they examine
them.   June 10, 1909

Illustration (2)

J. H. BROWN—Steamboat Pilot, Ohio Co., Ky.
Below knee.

I am pleased to say that I find great satisfaction in wearing your leg. I am a steamboat pilot, and sometimes stand on my feet for eighteen hours, walking a bridge or climbing a ladder just the same as I ever did. I would not be without one for ten times the cost of a leg, and I am ready and willing to give any information I can to anyone in need.

Illustration (3)

THOS. FERNEY—Signalman, Quebec.
Below knee.

I take pleasure in recommending your artificial limbs, especially for their durability. My leg is amputated six inches below the knee joint. I have worn one of your limbs since 1888. I am employed as a signalman, and attend to my duties without the least trouble.

Illustration (4)

PROF. F. JACOBY—New Haven Co., Conn.
Below knee.

I was a professional tight rope walker and aeronaut before I lost my leg, and I did not propose to allow the loss of a leg to compel me to seek another occupation. I can walk a tight rope nearly as well as ever I could.

Note.—The above illustration has been made from an instantaneous photograph taken of Professor Jacoby while performing on a tight rope. He is balancing entirely on his artificial leg; his natural foot is off the rope in the act of passing forward to take the next step.

Illustration (5)

Chapter 17

The Chicago Office Opportunity

The position in the Chicago office turned out to be perfect for me. They really needed additional help since a staff practitioner had left. The opening was for a practitioner who had prosthetic patient care experience. I was ready for it and upper management agreed. There were two good reasons why I accepted the new job. First, I would be exposed to many different types of prosthetic cases and would be able to expand my skills. Second, they offered more compensation. I really appreciated the moderate salary increase. I had learned a lot working in the Evansville branch office for almost two years, especially about upper extremity cases.

The manager, Mr. Burk, gave me all the cases that came in, except the patients who still wanted to wear wooden legs. I had no experience with that type of old style limb and I couldn't believe how many amputees still preferred that type of prosthetic device. The boss took those cases and the technician, Armand, helped him immensely, as they both had woodworking experience of that nature. They actually provided all types of prosthetic wood fabrication. I enjoyed watching them create the limbs from scratch and I learned so much about basic limb fabrication. It was like going back in time to the year 1910, as these types of limbs had been thought of as the highest of technical quality and achievement of the time. Armand fashioned a wooden foot with an articulating ankle joint that sat on leather bushings inside the freshly hand-carved wooden foot pieces. The toe bent with an insert of rubber that allowed a simulated toe flexing motion. These devices functioned as well as the modern type devices made with plastics, fiberglass, dacron, nylon, rubber and various metals instead of wood. The way these limbs performed was also impressive as the gait patterns were also so similar to the limbs we were making in the late 1970's.

There were two main reasons why doctors in the Chicago area were still prescribing the old-fashioned type limbs. First, patients insisted on that type of limb because they were used to it and trusted its comfort level and performance. Second, the thickness of the wood allowed the socket, the part of the artificial limb that the patient fits their remaining limb into, to be made bigger if the patient gained weight.

One day, Mrs. Serena, an elderly woman, came into the Chicago office with her son. I started making her what I thought would be a perfect artificial limb. After about sixteen hours of labor, going step by step as I had been taught, the leg was ready. Mrs. Serena returned for the dynamic alignment and then completion of the prosthesis. During the fitting she consistently complained about a pressure spot that was painfully annoying. I spent hours trying to relieve the pressure spot by grinding plastic away from the troublesome area. She pointed to a place on her amputated limb that seemed to cause the pain. On the inside of the socket that mirrored that spot, I sanded the socket; sure I had eased the imperfection, only to have her repeatedly tell me that it was still painful.

Sweat dripped off my pale face as I concentrated with immense intensity, desperately trying to find the mysterious area that was causing her such discomfort. I was at my wit's end and didn't know what to do. Mrs. Serena's son was getting tired of waiting and his impatience was obvious as he paced the room. I could not find the spot and I felt like I was also beginning to ruin the socket's overall fit with the continual grinding. I didn't want to ruin the rest of the fit and make the situation worse. If only I could mark the spot on her and transfer it to the inner socket of the artificial leg, I would then be able to solve the problem. It had become obvious that the area she indicated was not where the cause of the problem existed. With her permission, I pushed in different spots on her remaining limb to simulate the feeling she would have while standing on it. Mrs. Serena emitted a definite grimace when I found the exact sore spot. Once I had found it, I discovered that it was in a completely different location than where she had been pointing.

Now I had to mark it in a way that would transfer to the inside of the socket. The secretary in the front office looked at me strangely when I asked to borrow her lipstick for a minute. I used the lipstick to mark Mrs. Serena's amputated limb directly on the pressure spot I had found. I had her step into the limb for a few more painful seconds without her prosthetic sock on. I hoped that this would be the last time I would see her contorted facial expression of pain as I slipped the limb off. I apologized to her deeply again for all her trouble and she gave me a weak smile in return. I finally had an exact mark of the pressure spot in the socket and I took off for the grinding machine. I relieved the lipstick marked area by sanding just the lipstick marked region until I created a pressure relief spot. I scurried back, smiling, and put the limb on her and lo and behold no more pain. I had a successful fit, thank God. It was quite a learning experience and from then on lipstick was one of my most useful diagnostic tools.

Electronic limbs for the arms had just been invented and I had some great experiences providing these upper extremity devices. I learned a lot about arms while working in Chicago and provided many while I worked there. Chicago was highly industrialized and that led to approximately twenty percent of the practice being concentrated on upper extremity cases. Arms are somewhat easier to create than legs, mainly because you don't walk on your arms. There is a lot less pressure and stress on the amputated arm tissue versus the amputated lower limb tissue. The legs have to support your entire body weight and the pounds per square inch can really add up and cause some stress. Arms are also complicated to make but have different complications to deal with than lower limbs did.

I often remembered my upper extremity work experience from my first prosthetic facility in El Paso. I assisted in the fabrication of a relatively famous man's arms. His name was G. G. Armando, the private detective. He had lost both his hands and half his forearms below the elbow while playing with blasting Capps he had found near the railroad tracks where he lived. When he had been just twelve years old, he had blown his hands and arms up while trying to get the Capps to explode by smashing them between two rocks. He had a 22-caliber handgun mechanism manufactured to his specifications that he literally had us insert into his right prosthetic arm. It could fire just one shot at a time. It had a modified trigger in the form of a loop that was connected to his arm with a stainless steel cable. He could make it fire by tightening his biceps muscle that was attached to the other end of this stainless steel cable. That handgun mechanism was considered a concealed weapon and he was licensed to carry it because he was a private detective.

We were impressed, especially when he told us that he was invited to do an episode of the television series, *Hawaii Five-O*. The episode was called "Hook Man". I begged Armando for an autographed picture taken on the movie set and GG actually said he would take care of it for me. I still have it to this day, a signed black and white glossy picture of GG posing with Jack Lord, the star of *Hawaii Five-O*. The two men were pretending to be fist fighting and GG Armando signed it using one of his hooks. I will always appreciate how he signed it: "Kevin, always be tough, this is a tough world," with the year, 1973.

108

While I was working in Chicago, my parents decided to move to Florida. My brothers and I had all moved away from El Paso where we had lived for about fifteen years. My grandparents, Ida and Joe, who had been living in Cleveland, and my uncle Jack, who had lived in New Jersey, had already moved to Florida. They talked my parents into moving there as well. Growing up mostly in El Paso I had learned to love the warm weather. Waking up in the morning and going outside only to be greeted by warm air was something I realized I enjoyed and missed very much. I decided to move to Florida as soon as I could secure a good job. The cold weather of Chicago was not for me. My amputated limb in my plastic prosthesis would actually feel like it had been in a freezer after being outside in the snow for just a few minutes. I was ready to move after a couple of terrible winters and finally did so in the summer of 1980.

I drove down in a different car as I had wrecked my Corvette on the outer drive in Chicago during a snowstorm when I had become involved in a pile-up type accident as I drove over an ice-covered overpass. The accident hadn't been my fault, but I was heartbroken when I saw my car get smashed as the cars kept piling up. My car was totaled but at least I was able to sell it for parts and received about nine hundred dollars. I had to settle for an old yellow Cutlass Supreme because, as a learning prosthetist I was still on a rather modest salary. I drove down to sunny, warm Florida.

Because I was an amputee, I felt I had to learn to drive exceptionally well. I was always afraid of losing my driver's license because I thought that the police would think I was a hazardous driver if I was constantly involved in traffic accidents and they knew I was an amputee. My fears could be traced back to an incident that occurred one fine day in El Paso, when my boss had sent me on an errand in his station wagon.

I was stopped at an intersection. I was bored to death with this task, when I saw some ladies sitting and waiting for a bus across the street. It was a four-way stop. I decided to floor the gas pedal as I made a sharp left turn. The rear wheels emitted an ear-splitting screech that freaked out the ladies sitting on the corner. I had been totally enjoying testing my driving skills until a police officer who had witnessed the whole thing pulled me over. My heart was pounding! I felt I had to think of an excuse for what the officer had just witnessed. I could not afford to pay the ticket he was sure to issue me. The officer asked me to explain my actions, and as I was getting out of the car, I told him that I was driving my boss's car and I wasn't used to driving it. Finally, I added that I was an amputee. I told him that my foot had slipped off the brake and onto the gas pedal, causing the radical turn. To my surprise, he asked me to show him my artificial limb.

I was wearing a Vocational Rehabilitation prosthesis that I had colored purple with plastic boat pigment. When I pulled my pant leg up, the officer stared in shock and amazement as he gazed upon my purple artificial leg. After what seemed an eternity, he said he would let me go this time and not give me a ticket. He also went on to say that he was going to spread the word about me to his fellow officers in the city. He warned me that if anything like this happened again they would take my driver's license away for good. He totally freaked me out and scared the hell out of me. I never thought of that possibility. Losing my driver's license would ruin my life. I realized that I needed to be a smart and safe driver so I could always keep my driver's license. I bet the police officers had a laugh about the kid with the purple leg in the police department that night!

I finally had a great job waiting for me in South Florida and it was very close to the Ft. Lauderdale area where my family had settled. A new opportunity was

110

opening up for me to learn about and work with a very special group, the elderly population of amputees, retired people from around the country. Chicago had been a great learning environment for me and I benefited from that work experience greatly. I now already had seven years of experience behind me as a prosthetist and I was feeling more confident than ever before about my expertise as a young prosthetist. I also felt that I had a lot to offer my patients. I couldn't wait to start work at my new job.

Prosthetic foot fabrication of the early 1900's in the United States

Photo (1)

Below knee type prosthetic fabrication of the early 1900's in the United States

Photo (2)

Prosthetic knee fabrication of the early 1900's in the United States

Photo (3)

Above knee type prosthetic fabrication of the early 1900's in the United States

Photo (4)

Chapter 18

You Can't Put a Straight Leg on a Crooked Man

The patients in Florida were just as fascinating as those in the Midwest. One of the most memorable was Elbert, a big man who worked as a laborer in a polo stable in Boca Raton. He was absolutely the strongest man I had ever met before, solidly built with huge muscles. He was obviously not afraid of hard work. He had a short below-knee amputation on his right leg. I agreed to make him a replacement prosthesis which he badly needed. Elbert could not afford to have his artificial leg replaced on a regular basis. In fact, a charitable organization called the Barr Foundation had arranged for him to receive his new leg.

Through the years since his childhood, Elbert's leg had become bowed, curving in like a banana shape towards his other leg. This probably had occurred because he had been unable to replace his limbs as he lost the fit and kept walking on an improperly fitting leg for long periods of time. Over the years his limb adjusted the best it could. The human body is always changing but the artificial limb doesn't change along with the remaining limb. Fitting problems always develop over time.

One day as I proceeded to fit him with his new leg he asked, "Why is this artificial leg so damn crooked? Why does it look all bent like that?" Staring at his prosthesis, I thought for a few seconds and answered him sincerely, because he truly was concerned about his prosthetic leg's appearance. "Elbert," I said, looking him directly in the eye, "You can't put a straight leg on a crooked man!" He was quiet for a short time with a blank look on his face as he stared away from me, and then all of the sudden he just lit up, his face smiling. He began laughing and nodding his head. We had a great time joking around during that office visit.

I was feeling very good about how I was progressing as a prosthetist, caring and treating my patients very well with respectful concern; always being very professional. Prosthetic school gave me my educational base, but my patients were my real educators. They helped me develop a mental library of successful cases and experiences to draw from throughout my career. As similar cases came up along the way, I could then quickly provide a complicated limb. I rapidly became more adept at my craft, because I knew how to make limbs for difficult cases from my past experience. I really appreciated watching my skills grow.

I was so confident I could even test out jokes as I worked and see which ones the patients really liked. I like humor very much and I enjoy hearing my patients laugh. My humor is very dry, but my patients seem to appreciate it. One of my favorite joking comments I still use today is: I casually tell the patient not to do any walking until I return, as I walk back to the lab with their artificial foot in my hand. The patient, who is sitting in a chair at the end of the parallel walking bars with a footless artificial limb on, usually grins, happy to be able to laugh at his/her situation.

Probably the nicest comment ever made to me from one of my patients was a comment made by a local Orthodox Rabbi, Rabbi B. During one office visit he sat in front of me, quiet and saddened by the painful fit that had most recently developed on his right lower limb. He saw the perplexed look on my face as I wondered how I could possibly make his poor-fitting right prosthetic limb more comfortable for him. He had a busy day ahead and until arrangements could be made to start the manufacture of a new proper fitting one, this one had to work. In an astute, soft voice he said, "God made me this limb, (as he pointed to his left limb) and you made me this one, (as he pointed to the prosthesis) and you

122

can fix it!" What an astounding comment and testament to Rabbi B's trust in me. I became energized with his motivational words and somehow I figured out a combination of different adjustments that worked. I know Rabbi B always appreciates my prosthetic work. He makes sure I know this by thanking me most sincerely while giving me a handshake and a nod of his head.

One long workday I was finishing up with this nice young man, Bill, having successfully provided him with a new below-the-knee type prosthesis. His wife, Jane, was a psychologist. I learned this as we had become friendly and gotten to know each other during the frequent visits that are routine when providing a custom-made prosthetic device, especially if it's a complicated case. As Bill walked out of the fitting room on his new leg, with crutches, Jane asked him to wait for her in the lobby because she wanted to talk to me for a few minutes. He called out, "Okay," as he gingerly walked down the short hallway to the waiting room with a great big smile of success on his face.

I closed the door and Jane asked me if she could talk to me about Bill. I told her, "of course." Jane was very concerned about her thirty-four-year-old husband. She could see a change in him or rather in his behavior since the automobile accident. He had driven off the road because he had fallen asleep at the wheel and had collided into a concrete barrier at a high speed totally crushing his left leg well below the knee. Jane felt Bill was adjusting well to his new amputee status and his new prosthesis but seemed a bit agitated and abrupt with her and the two children at times. She wanted my advice as to what I find in my patients' behavior with regard to this initial adjustment period after limb loss.

I had been helping amputees deal with their amputations for ten years now, since I had started my career. I had helped them cope with the grief and terrible trauma of limb loss and rather successfully, I thought. I did this mostly by providing good reliable prosthetics. I thought for a few seconds and tried to figure out what I could say that would help her understand what an amputee goes through as they try to begin to accept all that has happened to them. I really wanted to help Jane understand what her husband was going through; she was very serious and intent on helping him all she could. I was just going to talk about the anxiety everyone feels because mostly they just don't know what to expect. I encourage them to ask questions and I answer them. This helps lower the anxiety level. Jane just couldn't wait for me to answer and looked directly into my eyes and asked me another question before I could answer the first one. "What did you feel, Kevin, when you woke up after the surgery and saw for the very first time that your right foot was amputated? When you actually saw that it was removed and gone from your body forever?"

I looked at her and said quite easily, "I just felt the tremendous pain from the actual surgical event and immediately asked for a pain shot." Jane looked me in the eye, slammed the table with her hand and shouted, "Didn't you feel angry as hell, Kevin; didn't you feel completely pissed off?" As she was shouting at me, I kind of went into a type of trance and to my great surprise I began to feel waves of emotion literally undulating through my entire body. I couldn't believe how I was reacting to her comments. I tried to talk and Jane said abruptly, "You need to allow yourself to fully express this feeling of anger, Kevin, completely, so you can become fully adjusted to the reality of the fact that you are an amputee now and always will be," she said. "I think Bill is not able to do this quite yet and it is so important that he does, but you certainly can Kevin, right?"

I just sat there as she went on to tell me that the feeling of profound anger that she just described to me was a very honest feeling for me and any amputee to have. It was very real, absolutely true and legitimate. She went on to say, "Kevin, don't you feel any anger about what happened to you when you were just seventeen years old?" She stared at me with those kind thoughtful eyes that actually had a twinkle of light, you know, like the eyes of an enlightened person. I said, with a weak smile, looking back at her, "Yes," I said, "I have had that feeling of anger trapped inside me for so many years that it has cobwebs all over it. I can now allow myself to really feel it, cleanse myself of it all, and let - it - go!" I told her that to my amazement I just realized that I had never allowed myself to fully accept the loss of my foot and also express the honest feeling of anger as to why this had to happen to me and did happen to me. As she got up to leave, Jane said, "You should just be honest with yourself, Kevin. Remember; we all have the right to feel healthy and happy inside, so choose to be happy, Kevin, and truly *be* happy! I will be patient with Bill because I know my husband very well; he will completely pull through this in time. He is a very strong determined man, and he's a survivor. Thanks, Kevin, we will see you in two weeks for the check-up appointment."

When Jane left the office I felt like I could never thank her enough for what she had just helped me to finally do at twenty eight years of age. After being an amputee for approximately ten years, I was finally ready to bear the honest truth of my destiny that I just couldn't do in my youth, *accept it all* in a healthy balanced way. I felt so good inside with this brand new experience that I had never had before. It was a feeling of space, a sort of opening up and a release of pressure, an unfolding. The anger had left me finally and in my mind it felt like a fresh space had been created there and was now available for me to put to good use, to grow into, as a person should. I felt free and it was absolutely amazing.

While riding home in my car after work, I realized that I had learned that day something new, something very important, something more. After all these years I thought I was in balance, you know walking well on two well-made straight legs. All these years I thought I was in perfect balance when I really wasn't! One leg was always very crooked and remained that way for years even after I thought time had straightened it and put me into perfect balance. Like Elbert, I couldn't understand why a straight leg wouldn't fit on a crooked man. I had been off balance and had refused to see it! I thought I had adjusted well to my problems, however, in reality I had never stopped being angry about them. That day I had learned that holding onto anger is very bad for one's soul. I promised myself never to do that again, no matter what else might happen to me as I went through my life. In the future, I would always remember this promise to myself and I would always work to let anger go. I also discovered that day what a feeling actually is and how powerful a thing a feeling really is, especially with regard to how it can affect your inner being. Feelings are neither right nor wrong, they are just feelings, but they are an important part of our individuality; they are what makes us who we are. To tell you the truth, I had never thought about feelings before that day in this deep kind of way. From now on, I resolved to be an even more sensitive person.

As I drove home after a most difficult trying day filled with very intense work, I knew I would always work hard to make all my dreams come true. I knew the direction I wanted to go in and I vowed never to let anyone or anything stop me from achieving this. My vision for my future was worth all my efforts and all my hard work because I had great dreams and goals and I knew that it all wouldn't happen by itself. I would always need to continue working very hard for it and you know what, just as I had those thoughts, all the freeway lights immediately came on all at once as far as I could see, even in the rear-view mirror. Wow, what a cool sight, seeing all of those lights coming on in an instant! Oh yes, I thought, my dreams will all be coming true, I know! I felt better; light always seems to help me feel better.

This is my true story, my story of survival, survival of a catastrophe that occurred in my blameless most sensitive youth. I never saw it coming, and even when I did, I had absolutely no way to prepare for it or deal with it. My past demonstrates a kind of power of self determination that was necessary for me to carry on and get through my life just the way that I wanted to. I sought very much to live as normal a life as humanly possible, you know, to just simply fit in and do well. This resolve enabled me to endure the terrible suffering that I was forced into and yet still become a successful man in spite of it. I simply chose to keep myself on a path of determined success, always working hard, always looking ahead and never giving up!

I learned not to dwell on everything I couldn't do but instead I chose to focus on everything I could do. I had absolutely no help from some individuals who actually stood directly in my way trying to hold me back but I simply chose not to let them block me from achieving my dreams. I overcame my fears with the greatest difficulty at times but this was actually the most rewarding of all my experiences, conquering my fears. All along the way I did have help from family and good, very good, friends who were so helpful and meaningful to me that I can't even put into words how greatly it was appreciated. I could summarize and just say that they were all gifts to me from God. Most important of all, I learned that the most central thing to always keep in my life was something very simple; to always protect my truly God-given happy spirit, in spite of all the sadness and problems that I had been through or may yet be faced with!

I believe things always have a way of working out! In fact, today I am the owner of a successful prosthetics practice, married to the woman of my dreams, and the father of five beautiful children.

The Beginning.

PHOTO AND ILLUSTRATION CREDITS

The illustrations (1, 2, 3, 4, 5) are modern renderings of the original illustrations from the "Manual of Artificial Limbs", by A.A. Marks, original publication in 1905. The patient testimonials are real and relate to each illustration. The illustrations were beautifully done by the thirteen year old daughter of one of my dear patients, and her daughter's name is:

Chaya Moushka Esther Malka Gottesfeld

The photos (1, 2, 3, 4) are taken from the 1906 publication: Where Winkley Artificial Limbs are Made.

The Winkley catalog was created, I am told, by the great grandfather of Mr. Greg Gruman, C.P., President of Winkley Orthopedic Labs.

I thank Greg for the honor of using these wonderful and priceless pictures in my book.

On the cover: Kevin S. Garrison and his youngest son Gabriel Jacob with their family pet, Cavalier King Charles Spaniel, Zackary.